Organization

FOR
KINGDOM-PREACHING
AND
DISCIPLE-MAKING

"This good news of the kingdom will be preached in all the inhabited earth for a witness to all the nations." "Go . . . and make disciples of people of all the nations, baptizing them . . . teaching them."—Matt. 24:14; 28:19, 20.

CONTENTS

COPYRIGHT, 1972
by
WATCH TOWER BIBLE AND TRACT SOCIETY
OF PENNSYLVANIA

PUBLISHERS
WATCHTOWER BIBLE AND TRACT SOCIETY
OF NEW YORK, INC.
INTERNATIONAL BIBLE STUDENTS ASSOCIATION
Brooklyn, New York, U.S.A.

Made in the United States of America

CHAPTER 1

THE WORK OF PREACHING AND DISCIPLE-MAKING

JEHOVAH has provided good news for mankind, and it is his will that people everywhere be given opportunity to hear it. Now, as the wicked system of things nears its finish, the time left in which to reach people of all nations with this good news is short. There is much to be done. It is a work for everyone who truly loves God and who loves his neighbor. Will you share in it?

Of course, service to God has always included such basic matters as clean living, loving care for the members of one's family, obedience to divine law and prayerful expressions of gratitude to our Creator. But at various times Jehovah has also given special assignments of work to his servants. Noah, for example, was instructed to build an ark and to be a "preacher of righteousness" at a time when the earth was filled with violence. Israel's prophets served as God's spokesmen, announcing both good news and messages of judgment. —2 Pet. 2:5; Gen. 6:13, 14; Jer. 1:7-10.

The special work assigned to Christians was begun at Jehovah's direction nineteen hundred years ago. It was a twofold work: first, that of proclaiming the good news of God's kingdom along with God's judgment messages to peoples of all nations, and, second, that of teaching all those people responding favorably to that proclamation, making disciples of them.

God gave a splendid start to that work, using his own Son to initiate it and to set the right pattern for others to follow. Jesus personally "set out on a tour of all the cities and villages, teaching in their synagogues and preaching the good

3

news of the kingdom." (Matt. 9:35) Those who became his disciples were given needed instruction and then were themselves sent into cities and villages.—Matt. 10:5-15; Luke 9:1-6; 10:1-16.

Though confining his own activity mainly to the nation of Israel, Jesus showed that the ministry of his followers would reach out "to the most distant part of the earth." (Acts 1:8) "This good news of the kingdom will be preached in all the inhabited earth for a witness to all the nations," he said, "and then the end will come." (Matt. 24:14) Before returning to the heavenly courts of his Father, Jesus commanded his disciples: "Go . . . and make disciples of people of all the nations, baptizing them in the name of the Father and of the Son and of the holy spirit, teaching them to observe all the things I have commanded you. And, look! I am with you all the days until the conclusion of the system of things." —Matt. 28:19, 20.

Rightly, this work would be intensified in our time, down here at the "conclusion of the system of things." The Scriptures, together with all the evidence in fulfillment of prophecy since 1914 C.E., show that Jehovah has 'taken his great power and begun to rule as king.' He has done so by conferring upon his Son Jesus Christ active ruling authority over the nations. (Rev. 11:15-18; Dan. 7:13, 14) The 'hour of judgment' has arrived, and people of all nations are being separated, with either survival or destruction in the coming "great tribulation" in view. God's angels have a share invisibly in directing this global work of separation, with its visible activity of Kingdom-preaching and disciple-making. Yes, God's universal family in heaven and on earth works unitedly to accomplish this mammoth task in harmony with the Father's will.—Rev. 14:6, 7; Matt. 13:40, 41, 49; 25:31-46.

This work and the limited time remaining for its accomplishment place a test upon all persons. How much does the kingdom of God's Son mean to us? Will we zealously publicize it, or will we show indifference? Will we boldly advocate it, or will we be shamefully silent about it? What we do will not escape the King's notice. (Luke 9:26) Jehovah is allowing us to show what the Kingdom means to us, and our response is decisive as to what the future holds for us individually.

WHY EACH SHOULD SHARE

We should each want to have as large a share as possible in this special work. On the one hand we should view it as a sacred duty, an obligation, a requirement on which our very lives depend. In view of our Lord's command, we can say as did the apostle Paul: "Necessity is laid upon me. Really, woe is me if I did not declare the good news!" (1 Cor. 9:16) We rightly are guided by the "fear of Jehovah" in this, for the Bible definitely links our making public expression of what is in our hearts with our gaining salvation. —Ps. 111:10; Rom. 10:8-10.

But the real question is, What is in our hearts? For out of the heart's abundance the mouth is bound to speak. (Luke 6:45) Do we see clearly how Kingdom-preaching and disciple-making relate to the supreme issue that Satan the Devil raised over the rightness of Jehovah's universal sovereignty? Do we see how God's name and honor are involved and the part that our keeping integrity and being wholeheartedly obedient to him serve in the vindication and sanctification of his name? Do we love the name of God, not just the name "Jehovah" itself but all that the name stands for—his righteousness, his justice, his power, his wisdom, his patience, his mercy and, above all, his love? Then our hearts will move us to stand up on behalf of this 'incomparable God' as Jehovah's Christian witnesses, not covering over his righteousness in our hearts nor hiding his loving-kindness and trueness from others.—Compare Psalm 40:5-10.

From our study of the Bible we have come to appreciate what God's kingdom really is—not an expression of God's power simply to display God's almightiness, but his provision for correcting injustices and removing all oppression. It will restore peace and unity in all God's universal family under his own Sovereign Headship, to the everlasting blessing of all who willingly submit to his Son's administration of matters and his carrying out of his Father's purposes. What righteous-hearted person would not be thrilled to share such good news with others?—Isa. 11:1-5, 9; Eph. 1:9, 10.

Jehovah has been long-suffering and patient in allowing this time before the "great tribulation" in order that the Kingdom-preaching and disciple-making work can be carried out. He "does not desire any to be destroyed but desires all to attain to repentance." So, too, mercy and love for our neighbor should move us to do all we can to aid others to become reconciled to God before he expresses his anger by destroying the wicked. (2 Pet. 3:8-10, 15; 2 Cor. 5:20; 6:1, 2) But "how will they call on him in whom they have not put faith? How, in turn, will they put faith in him of whom they have not heard? How, in turn, will they hear without someone to preach?" (Rom. 10:14) By responding to that need for preachers, making the life-giving message available to the greatest number possible, we can show that we are like our heavenly Father.—Eph. 4:32–5:2.

Feeling keenly the urgency of the times, we will proclaim Jehovah's "year of goodwill," urging persons to 'search for Jehovah while he may be found,' saying in effect: "Why should you die . . . cause a turning back and keep living." (Isa.

61:2; 55:6, 7; Ezek. 18:31, 32) By so doing we shall be free of bloodguilt before God and shall have the great joy of helping many persons to gain life in Jehovah's righteous new order, all to his praise and honor through his Son and our King, Jesus Christ.—Acts 18:6.

CHAPTER 2

THE ORGANIZATION THAT JEHOVAH IS USING

EVEN before Jesus returned to heaven he made it plain how this work of preaching and disciple-making was going to be accomplished world wide. He told his disciples: "You will receive power when the holy spirit arrives upon you, and you will be witnesses of me . . . to the most distant part of the earth." (Acts 1:8) The work of witnessing was not going to be done in their own strength. Both the direction and the power to carry the work to its completion would come from Jehovah God through his Son.

It is noteworthy that when the holy spirit was poured out upon Jesus' disciples at Jerusalem at the time of the festival of Pentecost of 33 C.E., "they were all together at the same place." (Acts 2:1-4) And thereafter, as the preaching of the good news spread out to other lands, congregations of believers were formed. These congregations did not operate independently, each one setting up its own standards. There was a 'oneness of spirit' among them and a loving concern for believers in other places. (Eph. 4:3-6; Rom. 15:26; 16:16; Phil. 4:21, 22) They worked in close association with one another. Appropriately the apostle Peter could refer to the faithful followers of God's Son as "the entire association of your brothers in the world."—1 Pet. 5:9.

This "association of your brothers" belonged to God. They are spoken of at Acts 20:28 as "the congregation of God, which he purchased with the blood of his own Son." As they carried on their activity they were called on to give evidence of their appreciation of this relationship. Whom did they obey? They had been taught by Jesus to preach about "the kingdom of the heavens," but did they really look to God in heaven for direction? (Matt. 10:7) Called up before the Jewish high court and ordered to stop preaching on the basis of the name of Jesus, the apostles made their position clear when they said: "We must obey God as ruler rather than men." (Acts 5:29) Fittingly, in prayer they addressed Jehovah as their "Sovereign Lord." (Acts 4:24) The attitude of true Christians has not changed since then. Jehovah's Christian witnesses in these "last days" continue to look to Jehovah as their Supreme Ruler. They recognize that the Bible is his inspired Word and they conform their activity to what it says.—2 Tim. 3:16, 17.

The Scriptures show that no man is the head of the organization that Jehovah is using to accomplish the work of Kingdom-preaching and disciple-making. And those associated with that organization are not to look to any human as their leader. (Matt. 23:10) They recognize Jesus Christ as the Head of the congregation. He is such, not because they selected him for that position, but because God himself appointed his Son to that office. (John 15:16) As the apostle Paul explains: "He also subjected all things under his feet, and made him head over all things to the congregation, which is his body."—Eph. 1:22, 23.

"THE FAITHFUL AND DISCREET SLAVE"

That congregation has been brought together for a purpose. And what is that purpose? It was readily apparent to observers in Jerusalem at the time of the formation of the Christian congregation. The observers said: "We hear them speaking . . . about the magnificent things of God." (Acts 2:11) To these Christian speakers as the spiritual "Israel of God" the words applied: " 'You are my witnesses,' is the utterance of Jehovah, 'even my servant whom I have chosen.' " (Isa. 43:10; Gal. 6:16) They were Jehovah's Christian witnesses. Collectively these witnesses are called God's "servant." Thus it is evident that they are the ones referred to by Jesus when he asked: "Who really is the faithful and discreet slave whom his master appointed over his domestics, to give them their food at the proper time?" (Matt. 24:45) From the time of the outpouring of the holy spirit after Jesus' return to heaven, that "servant" or "slave" class, also called "the faithful steward," proceeded to care for its appointed responsibility. (Luke 12:42-44) Spiritual "food at the proper time" was provided under the direction of the Master, Jesus Christ. Of course, not all members of the "slave" class wrote counsel to the congregations, and not all gave admonition in public discourses. (1 Tim. 2:12) But all did contribute in various ways to the spiritual upbuilding of the "domestics," the individual members of the congregation.—Eph. 4:16.

The total number of those making up the membership of the "body" of Christ, the spirit-begotten congregation, is stated to be 144,000 persons. These, when resurrected to the heavens, are to reign with Christ as kings and priests. (Rev. 7:4-8; 14:1-5; 20:4, 6) Evidences show we are in the time of the "harvest," the conclusion of the present system of things. The remaining ones of this number on earth today are therefore few. (Matt. 13:37-43) They are the nucleus around which a much larger number of honest-hearted persons have gathered. These latter ones are called by Jesus his "other sheep." (John 10:16) The Bible also designates them as a "great crowd," having the hope of everlasting life on earth as subjects of the Kingdom.—Rev. 7:9-17.

The remaining ones of Christ's spirit-anointed body members on earth constitute the "faithful and discreet slave" of today, and it is this class, as foretold at Matthew 24:47, that the Lord Jesus has appointed "over *all* his belongings" here on earth. So it is vital to work in close association with this "slave" class and to respond in a positive way to the counsel that you receive through it.

From among the members of that "faithful and discreet slave" class certain ones serve as a visible governing body. In the first century of our Common Era that visible governing body was made up of the apostles and other "older men" in the Jerusalem congregation. (Acts 15:2, 6, 23) When they were called on to make decisions affecting the lives and activity of God's people, they considered carefully what the Scriptures said about the matter, looked to God for the direction of his spirit, and then gave appropriate counsel. They also appointed men to responsible positions. (Acts 6:1-6) And they sent out members of the governing body and others on special assignments. (Acts 8:14, 15; 11:22; 15:22) Response to such oversight provided by the Master Jesus Christ through this visible agency resulted in continued increase, with God's blessing.—Acts 16:1-5; 1 Cor. 3:6, 7.

INSTRUMENTS USED BY THE "FAITHFUL AND DISCREET SLAVE" CLASS

In order to carry out the work of preaching and disciple-making most effectively under modern-day conditions, the "faithful and discreet slave" has organized various legal corporations, the principal one of which is the Watch Tower Bible and Tract Society of Pennsylvania. This Society, made up of dedicated, baptized Christians, is nonprofit and is completely devoted to advancing the interests of true worship in the earth. To facilitate its work world wide, the Society also has branch offices in various countries. All of these are subject to the "faithful and discreet slave" class and its governing body.

Throughout the territory supervised by the various branch offices of the Watch Tower Society are congregations of Jehovah's Christian witnesses. These are all organized in harmony with the arrangements set out in the Scriptures. These congregations have appointed elders, at present some of the anointed and some of the "other sheep," but all spiritually qualified men, who serve as overseers and spiritual shepherds of the flock of God entrusted to their care. (Acts 14:23; 20:17, 28; Titus 1:5) None of these elders is looked to as the head of the congregation; that is the position to which God has appointed Jesus Christ. Rather, the elders as a body work together to care for the flock under the direction of the Fine Shepherd, Jesus Christ. (1 Tim. 4:14; John 10:11) They well know that the flock is not theirs but God's, and they recognize their accountability to Jehovah. The result is a unified organization, one that upbuilds and refreshes its members and that serves for the accomplishment of the work that God has given it to perform.

RECOGNIZING GOD'S ARRANGEMENT

If you desire to serve Jehovah and to share in the work that he gives his people to do today, you need to associate with those whom God approves. Are you convinced that Jehovah is using an earthly organization of disciples of Jesus Christ, that the Christian congregation of anointed ones is indeed the appointed "slave" that has been entrusted with *all* the earthly interests of the Master Jesus Christ?

From your study of the Bible, you have come to know that, in order to please God, persons must imitate God's people ('my people') and 'get out of Babylon the Great,' the world empire of false religion. (Rev. 18:4) Honest-hearted persons also must follow the counsel written to the congregation of anointed Christians that says: "Get out from among them, and separate yourselves . . . and I will take you in." (2 Cor. 6:17) And where is he going to take them? Into association with "the congregation of the living God," which is referred to at 1 Timothy 3:15 as "a pillar and support of the truth." Those who make up this congregation of anointed Christians are also said to be a 'people for God's name,' and, as we have already noted from the Scriptures, they look to Christ as their heavenly Head.—Acts 15:14.

Which organization fits this description? Well, who are the people that hold firmly to the Bible, drawing all their beliefs from its pages and using it as their guide in all affairs of life? Who have truly proved themselves to be the 'people for God's name,' treating his name Jehovah with respect and making it known around the globe? Who really show their subjection to Jesus Christ as Head by doing the things that he commanded: preaching the good news of the Kingdom, making disciples of people of all nations, and loving one another as he loved them? (John 13:34, 35) You know the answer. It is the "faithful and discreet slave" class of anointed Christians, to whom the "great crowd" of "other sheep" are now being gathered by the "fine shepherd" Jesus Christ. —John 10:16.

So, if it is your sincere desire to serve our loving God and Father, Jehovah, you will want to show appreciation for the "faithful and discreet slave" class that he is using and work wholeheartedly under its direction.

CHAPTER 3

YOUR RELATIONSHIP WITH GOD

BY BIRTH we are creatures that have descended from Adam and Eve, who were created by Jehovah God through his only-begotten Son, Jesus Christ. What life we now have, even though accompanied by imperfection, we owe to God the Creator, the Universal Life-giver. God does not owe us a single thing. We do not have the right to demand from him a single thing. All the good things that we now possess we owe to him, and many or most of these things he has bestowed upon us without his first asking us to accept them. Other things, although God offers them to us out of his own generosity and mercy, it remains for us to accept or refuse. One of these things that we are allowed to accept or refuse is relationship with Him as God and Father. This is because we were not born into God's universal family of recognized children.

None of us can assume relationship as something that belongs to us by right in view of our being creatures for whose existence God is responsible. Relationship with Him calls for certain qualifications on our part. God does not force relationship with Himself upon us. He offers to us the opportunity to enter into recognized relationship with him, according to his own philanthropy or love of mankind. It is plainly stated: "When the kindness and the love for man on the part of our Savior, God, was manifested, owing to no works in righteousness that we had performed, but according to his mercy he saved us through the bath that brought us to life and through the making of us new by holy spirit. This spirit he poured out richly upon us through Jesus Christ our Savior, that, after being declared righteous by

13

virtue of the undeserved kindness of that one, we might become heirs according to a hope of everlasting life." (Titus 3:4-7, *Int*)* Thus God took the initial steps in opening the way for mankind to return to relationship with Him.

In order to avail itself of this divine provision for the restoration of mankind to relationship with God, mankind has to come to a knowledge of this provision. Knowing this, Jehovah God lovingly sends forth the knowledge by means of his approved proclaimers of the good news. "This is fine and acceptable in the sight of our Savior, God, whose will is that all sorts of men should be saved and come to an accurate knowledge of truth. For there is one God, and one mediator between God and men, a man, Christ Jesus, who gave himself a corresponding ransom for all—this is what is to be witnessed to at its own particular times." —1 Tim. 2:3-6.

What is the first step to be taken by one who comes to a knowledge of God's provision and thereby receives an invitation to take advantage of it? It is the step of repentance over one's sins. The apostle Paul mentioned this initial step. When speaking to pagan Greeks in their heathenish ignorance, he said: "True, God has overlooked the times of such ignorance, yet now he is telling mankind that they should all everywhere repent. Because he has set a day in which he purposes to judge the inhabited earth in righteousness by a man whom he has appointed, and he has furnished a guarantee to all men in that he has resurrected him from the dead." (Acts 17:30, 31) Since that inspired statement, God has continued to exercise patience in permitting wickedness among mankind. The apostle Peter tells us God's reason for such unusual patience, saying: "Jehovah is not slow respecting his promise, as some people consider slowness, but he is patient with you because he

---

* Abbreviations for Bible versions are explained on page 192.

does not desire any to be destroyed but desires all to attain to repentance."—2 Pet. 3:9.

At the end of the "seventy weeks" of years as foretold by Daniel the prophet, Jehovah God in his mercy opened the way for the non-Jews or Gentiles to enter into relationship with him as Christians. (Dan. 9:24-27) Jehovah was the One who sent the apostle Peter to the home of the Gentile Cornelius at Caesarea to preach the good news to him and to those gathered in the home. There, by the outpouring of his holy spirit, Jehovah gave evidence of his acceptance of believing Gentiles into relationship with himself. (Acts 10:1-48) It is evident that those believing Gentiles who received the holy spirit and got baptized in water had repented of their sins. That the Christianized Jews were surprised at the fact that Jehovah took the initiative and cleared the way for the uncircumcised Gentiles to receive the message of salvation and act upon it is indicated by the record. We read concerning what happened after the apostle Peter reported to his Christian brothers in Judea who were in a questioning attitude: "Now when they heard these things, they acquiesced, and they glorified God, saying: 'Well, then, God has granted repentance for the purpose of life to people of the nations also.'"—Acts 11:1-18.

Of course, those repentant Gentiles had to turn around in their course or be converted just as the believing Jews had been obliged to do. Prior to the end of the seventieth week of years, the apostle Peter had declared to natural circumcised Jews at the temple in Jerusalem: "In this way God has fulfilled the things he announced beforehand through the mouth of all the prophets, that his Christ would suffer. Repent, therefore, and turn around so as to get your sins blotted out, that seasons of refreshing may come from the person of Jehovah." (Acts 3:18, 19) After the end of the seventieth week of years in 36 C.E. the turning around or conversion of many Gentiles who heard the good news took place. The apostle Paul was largely used in this regard. We read, concerning the time that the congregation at Antioch of Syria sent Paul and Barnabas up to Jerusalem to get a decision on the question of circumcising believing Gentiles: "Accordingly, after being conducted part way by the congregation, these men continued on their way through both Phoenicia and Samaria, relating in detail the conversion of people of the nations, and they were causing great joy to all the brothers."—Acts 15:3.

As in the case of the Jews, the repentance of the Gentiles was toward Jehovah God. As Paul said: "I did not hold back from telling you any of the things that were profitable nor from teaching you publicly and from house to house. But I thoroughly bore witness both to Jews and to Greeks about repentance toward God and faith in our Lord Jesus." (Acts 20:20, 21) The repentance is toward God, and likewise the conversion or turning around is to God. "Turn around and I should heal them." (John 12:40; Acts 28:27; Isa. 6:9, 10) It is therefore apparent that repentance and conversion are necessary steps that a person who accepts the message of salvation must take toward entering into relationship with Jehovah God. But now a definite action must take place. What?

On the day of Pentecost of 33 C.E. the apostle Peter said to thousands of inquiring Jews: "Repent, and let each one of you be baptized in the name of Jesus Christ for forgiveness of your sins, and you will receive the free gift of the holy spirit." (Acts 2:38) In the preceding year Jesus Christ had told other inquiring Jews: "This is the work of God, that you exercise faith in him whom that One sent forth." (John 6:29) So the repentant, converted one needs to make a definite acceptance of Jesus as Jehovah's Messiah in order to do the "work of God." He must do this before he can be baptized in water in the name of Jesus Christ. What this accepting of Jesus Christ as one's Leader means, he himself told his apostles, saying: "If anyone wants to come after me, let him disown himself and pick up his torture stake and continually follow me." (Matt. 16:24) When anyone disowns himself, he discontinues claiming possession of himself. He renounces his claim upon himself in favor of someone else.

Whom does the prospective follower of Christ choose to be his owner and thenceforth confess, acknowledge and adhere to as his sole owner? It is Jehovah God, the heavenly Father of the Lord Jesus Christ. By thus disowning oneself in order to become a disciple and follower of the Son of God one hands oneself over to Jehovah God. One commits the ownership of oneself to Jehovah God. This, since the end of the seventy weeks of years in 36 C.E., is what we today call "dedication." One makes this dedication of oneself to Jehovah God through Jesus Christ, for it is through Jesus Christ that God takes over ownership of the dedicating one. Hence it is said to Christians in relationship with God: "You do not belong to yourselves, for you were bought with a price. By all means, glorify God in the body of you people." (1 Cor. 6:19, 20) That is why Christian overseers are commanded "to shepherd the congregation of God, which he purchased with the blood of his own Son."—Acts 20:28.

Only after a believer had made such a dedication of himself to Jehovah God and taken up the discipleship of Jesus Christ is the believer qualified to get baptized "in the name of the Father and of the Son" as well as of the holy spirit. (Matt. 28:19; Acts 19:5) Thus water baptism is a symbol of this dedication of oneself to Jehovah God through Jesus Christ, preceded by repentance and conversion. By pursuing this course, the dedicated, baptized believer comes into possession of a "good conscience" toward God. (1 Pet. 3:21) Such a one who has thus symbolized his disowning of himself now becomes a slave owned by God and a disciple of His Christ. He must continue to obey the command, of Romans 6:13: "Present yourselves to God as those alive from the dead, also your members to God as weapons of righteousness." Moffatt's Bible translation here uses the words "dedicate yourselves" instead of "present yourselves."

FOR THOSE CONSIDERING BAPTISM

If you have dedicated your life to the doing of Jehovah's will and are now contemplating baptism, you will be greatly aided by reading recent publications of the Watch Tower Society in addition to the book that you are currently studying. The elders of the congregation with which you are associated will gladly make recommendations to you of material that will be most helpful.

Before each assembly of Jehovah's Christian witnesses, the presiding overseer of the congregation will ascertain whether any associating with the congregation have dedicated their lives to Jehovah and now need to get baptized. He will arrange for meetings to be held with these candidates for immersion so that he, probably with the assistance of others of the local body of elders, can review with them the eighty questions presented in this chapter. The purpose of this is to help them to be sure that they really understand what the step of dedication and baptism means and includes. This also gives the congregation the assurance and confidence that those getting baptized truly understand what it means to be one of Jehovah's Christian witnesses and that they meet the Scriptural requirements.

If you are arranging to be immersed, get your affairs in order so as to be able to attend all these preliminary meetings for baptismal candidates. Review beforehand the questions provided, with their accompanying texts, looking up all scriptures cited but not quoted. Think about each question and the way the Scriptural information affects your life.

The material outlined on pages 19 to 52 may be divided among three or more sessions, as the presiding overseer, the chairman of the body of elders, considers best. Usually he will conduct one or more of the sessions, with others of the elders conducting the remaining ones. These meetings provide a fine opportunity for some of the body of elders to become acquainted with you, and whom you with them. They will be glad to help you with any points you do not fully understand, so feel free to ask them questions.

Review, now, the basic teachings of the Bible that follow, one at a time, and also try to express in your own words what these scriptures mean to you.

Who is the true God?

The Bible answers: "You, whose name is Jehovah, you alone are the Most High over all the earth." (Ps. 83:18) "Jehovah our God is one Jehovah." (Deut. 6:4; Mark 12:29) "God is a Spirit, and those worshiping him must worship with spirit and truth." (John 4:24) [Consider how this differs from local popular beliefs, whether of Christendom or of other religions.]

What kind of God is Jehovah?

"God is love." (1 John 4:8) "The Rock, perfect is his activity, for all his ways are justice. A God of faithfulness, with whom there is no injustice; righteous and upright is he." (Deut. 32:4) "O the depth of God's riches and wisdom and knowledge! How unsearchable his judgments are and past tracing out his ways are!" (Rom. 11:33) "O Sovereign Lord Jehovah! Here you yourself have made the heavens and the earth by your great power and by your outstretched arm. The whole matter is not too wonderful for you yourself." (Jer. 32:17) "No man has seen God at any time; the only-begotten god who is in the bosom position with the Father is the one that has explained him." (John 1:18) "Jehovah went passing by before his face and declaring: 'Jehovah, Jehovah, a God merciful and gracious, slow to anger and abundant in loving-kindness and truth, preserving loving-kindness for thousands, pardoning error and transgression and sin, but by no means will he give exemption from punishment.'" (Ex. 34:6, 7)

"Jehovah is not slow respecting his promise, as some people consider slowness, but he is patient with you because he does not desire any to be destroyed but desires all to attain to repentance." (2 Pet. 3:9) "Before the mountains themselves were born, or you proceeded to bring forth as with labor pains the earth and the productive land, even from time indefinite to time indefinite you are God." (Ps. 90:2)

What does it mean to know God?

"You have been shown, so as to know that Jehovah is the true God; there is no other besides him." (Deut. 4:35) "If, please, I have found favor in your eyes, make me know, please, your ways, that I may know you." (Ex. 33:13) "Those knowing your name will trust in you." (Ps. 9:10) (Compare 1 John 2:3-6.)

What does the Bible mean when it says that Jehovah requires our exclusive devotion?

"Jesus said to him: 'It is written, "It is Jehovah your God you must worship, and it is to him alone you must render sacred service."'" (Luke 4:8) "You must not make for yourself a carved image or a form like anything that is in the heavens above or that is on the earth underneath or that is in the waters under the earth. You must not bow down to them nor be induced to serve them, because I Jehovah your God am a God exacting exclusive devotion." (Ex. 20:4, 5)

How will Jehovah God sanctify his name? How can we have a share in it?

"I will bring myself into judgment with him, with pestilence and with blood; . . . And I shall certainly magnify myself and sanctify myself and make myself known before the eyes of many nations; and they will have to know that I am Jehovah." (Ezek. 38:22, 23) "You must pray, then, this way: 'Our Father in the heavens, let your name be sanctified.'" (Matt. 6:9) "Jehovah of armies—he is the One whom you should treat as holy." (Isa. 8:13) "I have glorified you on the earth . . . I have made your name manifest to the men you gave me out of the world." (John 17:4, 6) "Maintain your conduct fine among the nations, that, in the thing in which they are speaking against you as evildoers, they may as a result of your fine works of which they are eyewitnesses glorify God in the day for his inspection." (1 Pet 2:12) [Consider how one's conduct reflects on Jehovah's name.]

Who is Jesus Christ, and what is his position in relation to Jehovah God?

"Peter said: 'You are the Christ, the Son of the living God.'" (Matt. 16:16) "I am going my way to the Father, because the Father is greater than I am." (John 14:28) "He is the image of the invisible God, the firstborn of all creation; because by means of him all other things were created in the heavens and upon the earth, the things visible and the things invisible, no matter whether they are thrones or lordships or governments or authorities. All other things have been created through him and for him. Also, he is before all other things and by means of him all other things were made to exist." (Col. 1:15-17) "There is one God, and one mediator between God and men, a man, Christ Jesus." (1 Tim. 2:5) "Keep this mental attitude in you that was also in Christ Jesus, who, although he was existing in God's form, gave no consideration to a seizure, namely, that he should be equal to God. No, but he emptied himself and took a slave's form and came to be in the likeness of men. More than that, when he found himself in fashion as a man, he humbled himself and became obedient as far as death, yes, death on a torture stake. For this very reason also God exalted him to a superior position and kindly gave him the name that is above every other name, so that in the name of Jesus every knee should bend of those in heaven and those on earth and those under the ground, and every tongue should openly acknowledge that Jesus Christ is Lord to the glory of God the Father." (Phil. 2:5-11)

Why did Jesus die a sacrificial death?

"The Son of man came, not to be ministered to, but to minister and to give his soul a ransom in exchange for many." (Matt. 20:28) "We behold Jesus, who has been made a little lower than angels, crowned with glory and honor for having suffered death, that he by God's undeserved kindness might taste death for every man. . . . that through his death he might bring to nothing the one having the means to cause death, that is, the Devil; and that he might emancipate all those who for fear of death were subject to slavery all through their lives." (Heb. 2:9, 14, 15) "He beheld Jesus coming toward him, and he said: 'See, the Lamb of God that takes away the sin of the world!'" (John 1:29)

How is the ransom an expression of God's love for mankind?

"God recommends his own love to us in that, while we were yet sinners, Christ died for us." (Rom. 5:8) "By this the love of God was made manifest in our case, because God sent forth his only-begotten Son into the world that we might gain life through him. The love is in this respect, not that we have loved God, but that he loved us and sent forth his Son as a propitiatory sacrifice for our sins." (1 John 4:9, 10) "God loved the world so much that he gave his only-begotten Son, in order that everyone exercising faith in him might not be destroyed but have everlasting life." (John 3:16)

How does the ransom affect us as individuals?

"By means of him we have the release by ransom through the blood of that one, yes, the forgiveness of our trespasses, according to the riches of his undeserved kindness." (Eph. 1:7) "My little children, I am writing you these things that you may not commit a sin. And yet, if anyone does commit a sin, we have a helper with the Father, Jesus Christ, a righteous one. And he is a propitiatory sacrifice for our sins, yet not for ours only but also for the whole world's." (1 John 2:1, 2) "The love the Christ has compels us . . . he died for all that those who live might live no longer for themselves, but for him who died for them." (2 Cor. 5:14, 15) "He that exercises faith in the Son has everlasting life; he that disobeys the Son will not see life, but the wrath of God remains upon him." (John 3:36)

What is the holy spirit?

"God's *active force* was moving to and fro over the surface of the waters." (Gen. 1:2) "You will receive power when the holy spirit arrives upon you, and you will be witnesses of me both in Jerusalem and in all Judea and Samaria and to the most distant part of the earth." (Acts 1:8) "They all became filled with holy spirit and started to speak with different tongues, just

as the spirit was granting them to make utterance."
(Acts 2:4)

How can we benefit from the operation of that spirit today?

"If you, although being wicked, know how to give good gifts to your children, how much more so will the Father in heaven give holy spirit to those asking him!" (Luke 11:13) "All Scripture is *inspired* of God and beneficial for teaching, for reproving, for setting things straight, for disciplining in righteousness." (2 Tim. 3:16; see also 2 Peter 1:21.) "Pay attention to yourselves and to all the flock, among which the holy spirit has appointed you overseers, to shepherd the congregation of God, which he purchased with the blood of his own Son." (Acts 20:28)

Whose ideas are recorded in the Bible? Does that mean that God personally spoke or wrote it all? Is all of it true?

"All Scripture is inspired of God." (2 Tim. 3:16) "That is why we also thank God incessantly, because when you received God's word, which you heard from us, you accepted it, not as the word of men, but, just as it truthfully is, as the word of God, which is also at work in you believers." (1 Thess. 2:13) "You know this first, that no prophecy of Scripture springs from any private interpretation. For prophecy was at no time brought by man's will, but men spoke from God as they were borne along by holy spirit." (2 Pet. 1:20, 21) "Sanctify them by means of the truth; your word is truth." (John 17:17)

Why should we pray, to whom, and how often?

"The end of all things has drawn close. Be sound in mind, therefore, and be vigilant with a view to prayers." (1 Pet. 4:7) "He went on to tell them . . . always to pray and not to give up." (Luke 18:1) "Pray for one another . . . A righteous man's supplication, when it is at work, has much force." (Jas. 5:16) "If you ask the Father for anything he will give it to you in my name. . . . Ask and you will receive, that your joy may be made full." (John 16:23, 24) "To my sayings do give ear, O Jehovah; do understand my sighing. Do pay attention to the sound of my cry for help, O my King and my God, because to you I pray." (Ps. 5:1, 2)

"Pray incessantly." (1 Thess. 5:17) "Persevere in prayer." (Rom. 12:12)

About what is it proper to pray?

"No matter what it is that we ask according to his will, he hears us." (1 John 5:14) "Do not be anxious over anything, but in everything by prayer and supplication along with thanksgiving let your petitions be made known to God." (Phil. 4:6) "In the name of our Lord Jesus Christ giving thanks always for all things to our God and Father." (Eph. 5:20) "You must pray, then, this way: 'Our Father in the heavens, let your name be sanctified. Let your kingdom come. Let your will take place, as in heaven, also upon earth. Give us today our bread for this day; and forgive us our debts, as we also have forgiven our debtors. And do not bring us into temptation, but deliver us from the wicked one.'" (Matt. 6:9-13)

What is the kingdom of God?

"With the clouds of the heavens someone like a son of man happened to be coming; and to the Ancient of Days he gained access, and they brought him up close even before that One. And to him there were given rulership and dignity and kingdom, that the peoples, national groups and languages should all serve even him. His rulership is an indefinitely lasting rulership that will not pass away, and his kingdom one that will not be brought to ruin." (Dan. 7:13, 14) "Jesus answered: 'My kingdom is no part of this world. If my kingdom were part of this world, my attendants would have fought that I should not be delivered up to the Jews. But, as it is, my kingdom is not from this source.'" (John 18:36) "They sing a new song, saying: 'You are worthy to take the scroll and open its seals, because you were slaughtered and with your blood you bought persons for God out of every tribe and tongue and people and nation, and you made them to be a kingdom and priests to our God, and they are to rule as kings over the earth.'" (Rev. 5:9, 10)

What does it mean to 'seek first the kingdom'?

"Stop storing up for yourselves treasures upon the earth, where moth and rust consume, and where thieves

break in and steal. Rather, store up for yourselves
treasures in heaven, where neither moth nor rust con-
sumes, and where thieves do not break in and steal. . . .
No one can slave for two masters; for either he will
hate the one and love the other, or he will stick to the
one and despise the other. You cannot slave for God
and for Riches. . . . So never be anxious and say, 'What
are we to eat?' or, 'What are we to drink?' or, 'What
are we to put on?' For all these are the things the
nations are eagerly pursuing. For your heavenly Father
knows you need all these things. Keep on, then, seeking
first the kingdom and his righteousness, and all these
other things will be added to you." (Matt. 6:19-33) "So,
then, because we have so great a cloud of witnesses
surrounding us, let us also put off every weight and
the sin that easily entangles us, and let us run with
endurance the race that is set before us, as we look
intently at the Chief Agent and Perfecter of our faith,
Jesus. For the joy that was set before him he endured
a torture stake, despising shame, and has sat down
at the right hand of the throne of God. Indeed, consider closely the one who has endured such contrary
talk by sinners against their own interests, that you
may not get tired and give out in your souls." (Heb.
12:1-3) "This good news of the kingdom will be preached
in all the inhabited earth for a witness to all the
nations; and then the end will come." (Matt. 24:14)

When Christ returns, is it visibly as a man, or how?

  "When the Son of man arrives in his glory, and all
the angels with him, then he will sit down on his glorious throne." (Matt. 25:31) "Christ died once for all
time concerning sins, a righteous person for unrighteous ones, that he might lead you to God, he being
put to death in the flesh, but being made alive in the
spirit." (1 Pet. 3:18) "In the house of my Father there
are many abodes. Otherwise, I would have told you,
because I am going my way to prepare a place for you.
Also, if I go my way and prepare a place for you, I
am coming again and will receive you home to myself,
that where I am you also may be. A little longer and
the world will behold me no more, but you will behold
me, because I live and you will live." (John 14:2, 3, 19)

How can people know when his second presence occurs?

Read in the Bible the entire chapters of Matthew 24, 25; Mark 13; Luke 21; Daniel 4; Revelation 6.

What is God's purpose for the earth?

"God blessed them and God said to them: 'Be fruitful and become many and fill the earth and subdue it, and have in subjection the fish of the sea and the flying creatures of the heavens and every living creature that is moving upon the earth.'" (Gen. 1:28) "He has founded the earth upon its established places; it will not be made to totter to time indefinite, or forever." (Ps. 104:5) "As regards the heavens, to Jehovah the heavens belong, but the earth he has given to the sons of men." (Ps. 115:16) "Let your kingdom come. Let your will take place, as in heaven, also upon earth." (Matt. 6:10)

How will this purpose be realized?

"In the days of those kings the God of heaven will set up a kingdom that will never be brought to ruin. And the kingdom itself will not be passed on to any other people. It will crush and put an end to all these kingdoms, and it itself will stand to times indefinite." (Dan. 2:44) "We thank you, Jehovah God, the Almighty, the One who is and who was, because you have taken your great power and begun ruling as king. But the nations became wrathful, and your own wrath came, and the appointed time for the dead to be judged, and to give their reward to your slaves the prophets and to the holy ones and to those fearing your name, the small and the great, and to bring to ruin those ruining the earth." (Rev. 11:17, 18)

What conditions will prevail on earth in God's new system of things?

"There are new heavens and a new earth that we are awaiting according to his promise, and in these righteousness is to dwell." (2 Pet. 3:13) "I saw a new heaven and a new earth; for the former heaven and the former earth had passed away, and the sea is no more. I saw also the holy city, New Jerusalem, coming down out of heaven from God and prepared as a bride adorned for her husband. With that I heard a loud voice from the throne say: 'Look! The tent of God is with mankind, and he will reside with them, and they will be his peoples. And God himself will be with them. And he will wipe out every tear from their eyes, and death will be no more, neither will mourning nor outcry nor pain be anymore. The former things have passed away.'" (Rev. 21:1-4) "There must go forth a twig out of the stump of Jesse; and out of his roots a sprout will be fruitful. And upon him the spirit of Jehovah must settle down, the spirit of wisdom and of understanding, the spirit of counsel and of mightiness, the spirit of knowledge and of the fear of Jehovah; and there will be enjoyment by him in the fear of Jehovah. And he will not judge by any mere appearance to his eyes, nor reprove simply according to the thing heard by his ears. And with righteousness he must judge the lowly ones, and with uprightness he must give reproof in behalf of the meek ones of the earth. And he must strike the earth with the rod of his mouth; and with the spirit of his lips he will put the wicked one to death. And righteousness must prove to be the belt of his hips, and faithfulness the belt of his loins. And the wolf will actually reside for a while with the male lamb, and with the kid the leopard itself will lie down, and the calf and the maned young lion and the well-fed animal all together; and a mere little boy will be leader over them. And the cow and the bear themselves will feed; together their young ones will lie down. And even the lion will eat straw just like the bull. And the sucking child will certainly play upon the hole of the cobra; and upon the light aperture of a poisonous snake will a weaned child actually put his own hand. They will not do any harm or cause any ruin in all my holy mountain; because the earth will certainly be filled with the knowledge of Jehovah as the waters are covering the very sea." (Isa. 11:1-9) "He will actually swallow up death forever, and the Sovereign Lord Jehovah will certainly wipe the tears from all faces. And the reproach of his people he will take away from all the earth, for Jehovah himself has spoken it." (Isa. 25:8) "The earth itself will certainly give its produce; God, our God, will bless us." (Ps. 67:6) "Come, you people, behold the activities of Jehovah, how he has set astonishing events on the earth. He is making wars to cease to the extremity of the earth." (Ps. 46:8, 9)

Who is the Devil? What is his origin?

"Now the serpent proved to be the most cautious of all the wild beasts of the field that Jehovah God had made. So it began to say to the woman: 'Is it really so that God said you must not eat from every tree of the garden?' At this the woman said to the serpent: 'Of the fruit of the trees of the garden we may eat. But as for eating of the fruit of the tree that is in the middle of the garden, God has said, "You must not eat from it, no, you must not touch it that you do not die."' At this the serpent said to the woman: 'You positively will not die. For God knows that in the very day of your eating from it your eyes are bound to be opened and you are bound to be like God, knowing good and bad.'" (Gen. 3:1-5) "So down the great dragon was hurled, the original serpent, the one called Devil and Satan, who is misleading the entire inhabited earth; he was hurled down to the earth, and his angels were hurled down with him." (Rev. 12:9) "Put on the complete suit of armor from God that you may be able to stand firm against the machinations of the Devil; because we have a wrestling, not against blood and flesh, but . . . against the wicked spirit forces in the heavenly places." (Eph. 6:11, 12)

Against what spiritistic practices employed by the Devil and his demons does the Bible warn us?

"There should not be found in you anyone who . . . employs divination, a practicer of magic or anyone who looks for omens or a sorcerer, or one who binds others with a spell or anyone who consults a spirit medium or a professional foreteller of events or anyone who inquires of the dead." (Deut. 18:10, 11) "As we were going to the place of prayer, a certain servant girl with a spirit, a demon of divination, met us. She used to furnish her masters with much gain by practicing the art of prediction." (Acts 16:16) [List practices that are prevalent in your locality.]

How can we protect ourselves against the influence of these wicked spirits?

"Subject yourselves, therefore, to God; but oppose the Devil, and he will flee from you." (Jas. 4:7) "Put on the complete suit of armor from God that you may be able to stand firm against the machinations of the Devil . . .

On this account take up the complete suit of armor from God, that you may be able to resist in the wicked day and, after you have done all things thoroughly, to stand firm. Stand firm, therefore, with your loins girded about with truth, and having on the breastplate of righteousness, and with your feet shod with the equipment of the good news of peace. Above all things, take up the large shield of faith, with which you will be able to quench all the wicked one's burning missiles. Also, accept the helmet of salvation, and the sword of the spirit, that is, God's word, while with every form of prayer and supplication you carry on prayer on every occasion in spirit." (Eph. 6:11-18)

Why has God permitted wickedness to continue until now?

"What shall we say, then? Is there injustice with God? Never may that become so! For he says to Moses: 'I will have mercy upon whomever I do have mercy, and I will show compassion to whomever I do show compassion.' So, then, it depends, not upon the one wishing nor upon the one running, but upon God, who has mercy. For the Scripture says to Pharaoh: 'For this very cause I have let you remain, that in connection with you I may show my power, and that my name may be declared in all the earth.' So, then, upon whom he wishes he has mercy, but whom he wishes he lets become obstinate. . . . God, although having the will to demonstrate his wrath and to make his power known, tolerated with much long-suffering vessels of wrath made fit for destruction, in order that he might make known the riches of his glory upon vessels of mercy, which he prepared beforehand for glory." (Rom. 9:14-23; see also Job 1:9-12; 2:4-6.) "Jehovah is not slow respecting his promise, as some people consider slowness, but he is patient with you because he does not desire any to be destroyed but desires all to attain to repentance. Furthermore, consider the patience of our Lord as salvation, just as our beloved brother Paul according to the wisdom given him also wrote you." (2 Pet. 3:9, 15)

By what means will God destroy the wicked?

"The ten horns that you saw, and the wild beast, these will hate the harlot and will make her devastated and naked, and will eat up her fleshy parts and will completely burn her with fire. For God put it into their hearts to carry out his thought." (Rev. 17:16, 17) "In one day her plagues will come, death and mourning and famine, and she will be completely burned with fire, because Jehovah God, who judged her, is strong." (Rev. 18:8) "I saw the heaven opened, and, look! a white horse. And the one seated upon it is called Faithful and True, and he judges and carries on war in righteousness. And out of his mouth there protrudes a sharp long sword, that he may strike the nations with it, and he will shepherd them with a rod of iron. He treads too the winepress of the anger of the wrath of God the Almighty. And I saw the wild beast and the kings of the earth and their armies gathered together to wage the war with the one seated on the horse and with his army. And the wild beast was caught, and along with it the false prophet that performed in front of it the signs with which he misled those who received the mark of the wild beast and those who render worship to its image. While still alive, they both were hurled into the fiery lake that burns with sulphur. But the rest were killed off with the long sword of the one seated on the horse, which sword proceeded out of his mouth. And all the birds were filled from the fleshy parts of them." (Rev. 19:11, 15, 19-21) "I saw an angel coming down out of heaven with the key of the abyss and a great chain in his hand. And he seized the dragon, the original serpent, who is the Devil and Satan, and bound him for a thousand years. And he hurled him into the abyss and shut it and sealed it over him, that he might not mislead the nations anymore until the thousand years were ended. After these things he must be let loose for a little while. Now as soon as the thousand years have been ended, Satan will be let loose out of his prison, and he will go out to mislead those nations in the four corners of the earth, Gog and Magog, to gather them together for the war. The number of these is as the sand of the sea. And the Devil who was misleading them was hurled into the lake of fire and sulphur, where both the wild beast and the false prophet already were." (Rev. 20:1-3, 7, 8, 10)

What is the human soul? Can it die?

"Jehovah God proceeded to form the man out of dust from the ground and to blow into his nostrils the breath of life, and the man came to be a living soul." (Gen. 2:7; see also 1 Corinthians 15:45.) "Look! All the souls—to me they belong. As the soul of the father so likewise the soul of the son—to me they belong. The soul that is sinning—it itself will die." (Ezek. 18:4, 20) "Indeed, any soul that does not listen to that Prophet will be completely destroyed from among the people." (Acts 3:23)

What is sin, and how did we all become sinners?

"Everyone who practices sin is also practicing lawlessness, and so sin is lawlessness." (1 John 3:4) "All have sinned and fall short of the glory of God." (Rom. 3:23) "Through one man sin entered into the world and death through sin, and thus death spread to all men because they had all sinned." (Rom. 5:12) "If we make the statement: 'We have no sin,' we are misleading ourselves and the truth is not in us." (1 John 1:8) "There is no man that does not sin." (1 Ki. 8:46)

What should be our attitude toward committing sins?

"Do not let sin continue to rule as king in your mortal bodies that you should obey their desires. Neither go on presenting your members to sin as weapons of unrighteousness, but present yourselves to God as those alive from the dead, also your members to God as weapons of righteousness. For sin must not be master over you, seeing that you are not under law but under undeserved kindness." (Rom. 6:12-14)

Do only those who have committed gross sins or flagrant violations of God's Word need to repent?

"God . . . is telling mankind that they should all everywhere repent." (Acts 17:30) "Do you not know that the friendship with the world is enmity with God? Whoever, therefore, wants to be a friend of the world is constituting himself an enemy of God." (Jas. 4:4) "The chief priests and the older men of the people came up to him while he was teaching . . . Jesus said to them: 'Truly I say to you that the tax collectors and the harlots are going ahead of you into the kingdom of God. For John came to you in a way of righteousness, but you did not believe him. However, the tax collectors and the harlots believed him, and you, although you saw this, did not feel regret afterwards so as to believe him.' " (Matt. 21:23, 31, 32) "I went bringing the message that they should repent and turn to God by doing works that befit repentance." (Acts 26:20)

What is death?

"He said to them: 'Lazarus our friend has gone to rest, but I am journeying there to awaken him from sleep.' Therefore the disciples said to him: 'Lord, if he has gone to rest, he will get well.' Jesus had spoken, however, about his death. But they imagined he was speaking about taking rest in sleep. At that time, therefore, Jesus said to them outspokenly: 'Lazarus has died.' " (John 11:11-14) "The living are conscious that they will die; but as for the dead, they are conscious of nothing at all, neither do they anymore have wages, because the remembrance of them has been forgotten. All that your hand finds to do, do with your very power, for there is no work nor devising nor knowledge nor wisdom in Sheol, the place to which you are going." (Eccl. 9:5, 10) "In the sweat of your face you will eat bread until you return to the ground, for out of it you were taken. For dust you are and to dust you will return." (Gen. 3:19)

Why do people die?

"The wages sin pays is death." (Rom. 6:23) "In Adam all are dying." (1 Cor. 15:22)

What future hope for life is there for one who dies?

"I have hope toward God, which hope these men themselves also entertain, that there is going to be a resurrection of both the righteous and the unrighteous." (Acts 24:15) "Do not marvel at this, because the hour is coming in which all those in the memorial tombs will hear his voice and come out, those who did good things to a resurrection of life, those who practiced vile things to a resurrection of judgment." (John 5:28, 29) "The sea gave up those dead in it, and death and Hades gave up those dead in them, and they were judged individually according to their deeds." (Rev. 20:13)

How many from among mankind will be in heaven with Christ?

"I saw, and, look! the Lamb standing upon the Mount Zion, and with him a hundred and forty-four thousand having his name and the name of his Father written on their foreheads. And they are singing as if a new song before the throne and before the four living creatures and the elders; and no one was able to master that song but the hundred and forty-four thousand, who have been bought from the earth." (Rev. 14:1, 3; see also 7:4-8.)

What will they do there?

"You made them to be a kingdom and priests to our God, and they are to rule as kings over the earth." (Rev. 5:10) "I saw thrones, and there were those who sat down on them, and power of judging was given them. Yes, I saw the souls of those executed with the ax for the witness they bore to Jesus and for speaking about God, and those who had worshiped neither the wild beast nor its image and who had not received the mark upon their forehead and upon their hand. And they came to life and ruled as kings with the Christ for a thousand years. Happy and holy is anyone having part in the first resurrection; over these the second death has no authority, but they will be priests of God and of the Christ, and will rule as kings with him for the thousand years." (Rev. 20:4, 6)

Are Christians under the law covenant with its requirements of sabbath keeping and sacrifice?

"Christ is the end of the Law, so that everyone exercising faith may have righteousness." (Rom. 10:4) "The Law has become our tutor leading to Christ, that we might be declared righteous due to faith. But now that the faith has arrived, we are no longer under a tutor." (Gal. 3:24, 25) "Therefore let no man judge you in eating and drinking or in respect of a festival or of an observance of the new moon or of a sabbath; for those things are a shadow of the things to come, but the reality belongs to the Christ." (Col. 2:16, 17)

What Christian quality should outstandingly characterize our relationship with our spiritual brothers and with the members of our own families?

"I am giving you a new commandment, that you love one another; just as I have loved you, that you also love one another. By this all will know that you are my disciples, if you have love among yourselves." (John

13:34, 35) "Husbands, continue loving your wives, just as the Christ also loved the congregation and delivered up himself for it." (Eph. 5:25) "Recall the young women to their senses to love their husbands, to love their children." (Titus 2:4) "Continue putting up with one another and forgiving one another freely if anyone has a cause for complaint against another. Even as Jehovah freely forgave you, so do you also. But, besides all these things, clothe yourselves with love, for it is a perfect bond of union." (Col. 3:13, 14)

In God's arrangement, who is head of a married woman?

"You wives, be in subjection to your husbands, as it is becoming in the Lord." (Col. 3:18) "Let wives be in subjection to their husbands as to the Lord, because a husband is head of his wife as the Christ also is head of the congregation, he being a savior of this body." (Eph. 5:22, 23)

How should a husband exercise his headship?

"Husbands ought to be loving their wives as their own bodies. He who loves his wife loves himself." (Eph. 5:28) "You husbands, keep on loving your wives and do not be bitterly angry with them." (Col. 3:19) "You husbands, continue dwelling in like manner with them according to knowledge, assigning them honor as to a weaker vessel, the feminine one, since you are also heirs with them of the undeserved favor of life, in order for your prayers not to be hindered." (1 Pet. 3:7)

Is the wife whose husband is not a believer freed from his headship?

"You wives, be in subjection to your own husbands, in order that, if any are not obedient to the word, they may be won without a word through the conduct of their wives, because of having been eyewitnesses of your chaste conduct together with deep respect." (1 Pet. 3:1, 2) "A married woman is bound by law to her husband while he is alive; but if her husband dies, she is discharged from the law of her husband." (Rom. 7:2)

Who is responsible before God for the training and disciplining of children?

"You, fathers, do not be irritating your children, but go on bringing them up in the discipline and mental-regulating of Jehovah." (Eph. 6:4) "The one holding back his rod is hating his son, but the one loving him is he that does look for him with discipline." (Prov. 13: 24) "The rod and reproof are what give wisdom; but a boy let on the loose will be causing his mother shame." (Prov. 29:15) (See also Deuteronomy 6:6, 7.)

May a Christian have more than one living marriage mate?

" 'A man will leave his father and his mother and will stick to his wife, and the two will be one flesh' . . . So that they are no longer two, but one flesh." (Matt. 19:5, 6) "The overseer should therefore be irreprehensible, a husband of one wife." (1 Tim. 3:2, 12)

What is the only Scriptural basis for divorce that frees one to remarry?

"I say to you that whoever divorces his wife, except on the ground of fornication, and marries another commits adultery." (Matt. 19:9) "Everyone divorcing his wife, except on account of fornication, makes her a subject for adultery, and whoever marries a divorced woman commits adultery." (Matt. 5:32)

Must persons living together as husband and wife have their marriage legally registered with the government?

"Let marriage be honorable among all, and the marriage bed be without defilement, for God will judge fornicators and adulterers." (Heb. 13:4) "Continue reminding them to be in subjection and be obedient to governments and authorities as rulers, to be ready for every good work." (Titus 3:1) "Now in those days a decree went forth . . . for all the inhabited earth to be registered . . . Of course, Joseph also went up from Galilee . . . to get registered with Mary, who had been given him in marriage." (Luke 2:1-5)

Why must lying be avoided?

"The Devil . . . did not stand fast in the truth, because truth is not in him. When he speaks the lie, he speaks according to his own disposition, because he is a liar and the father of the lie." (John 8:44) "Jehovah does hate . . . a false tongue, and . . . a false witness that launches forth lies." (Prov. 6:16-19) "As for . . . all the liars, their portion will be in the lake that burns with

fire and sulphur. This means the second death."
(Rev. 21:8)

What is the Christian view of stealing?

"Let none of you suffer as a murderer or a thief."
(1 Pet. 4:15) "Let the stealer steal no more, but rather
let him do hard work, doing with his hands what is
good work, that he may have something to distribute to
someone in need." (Eph. 4:28)

What is the Christian view of drunkenness?

"What! Do you not know that unrighteous persons
will not inherit God's kingdom? Do not be misled.
Neither fornicators, nor idolaters, nor adulterers, . . .
nor greedy persons, nor drunkards . . . will inherit God's
kingdom." (1 Cor. 6:9, 10) "Ministerial servants should
likewise be serious, . . . not giving themselves to a lot
of wine." (1 Tim. 3:8)

What is God's law concerning blood?

"Every moving animal that is alive may serve as
food for you. As in the case of green vegetation, I do
give it all to you. Only flesh with its soul—its blood—
you must not eat." (Gen. 9:3, 4; see also Deuteronomy
12:15, 16.) "The holy spirit and we ourselves have
favored adding no further burden to you, except these
necessary things, to keep abstaining from things
sacrificed to idols and from blood and from things
strangled and from fornication. If you carefully keep
yourselves from these things, you will prosper. Good
health to you!" (Acts 15:28, 29) [List local practices
that are affected by this law.]

**What does the Bible say about fornication, adultery,
sexual relations with another person of the same sex and
other loose conduct? May a person who is engaging in
such practices be baptized?**

"Now the works of the flesh are manifest, and they
are fornication, uncleanness, loose conduct, idolatry,
practice of spiritism, enmities, strife, jealousy, fits of
anger, contentions, divisions, sects, envies, drunken
bouts, revelries, and things like these. As to these things
I am forewarning you, the same way as I did forewarn
you, that those who practice such things will not inherit God's kingdom." (Gal. 5:19-21) "Let marriage

be honorable among all, and the marriage bed be without defilement, for God will judge fornicators and adulterers." (Heb. 13:4) "Therefore God, in keeping with the desires of their hearts, gave them up to uncleanness, that their bodies might be dishonored among them, even those who exchanged the truth of God for the lie and venerated and rendered sacred service to the creation rather than the One who created, who is blessed forever. Amen. That is why God gave them up to disgraceful sexual appetites, for both their females changed the natural use of themselves into one contrary to nature; and likewise even the males left the natural use of the female and became violently inflamed in their lust toward one another, males with males, working what is obscene and receiving in themselves the full recompense, which was due for their error." (Rom. 1:24-27) "Deaden, therefore, your body members that are upon the earth as respects fornication, uncleanness, sexual appetite, hurtful desire, and covetousness, which is idolatry. On account of those things the wrath of God is coming. In those very things you, too, once walked when you used to live in them. But now really put them all away from you, wrath, anger, badness, abusive speech, and obscene talk out of your mouth. Do not be lying to one another. Strip off the old personality with its practices, and clothe yourselves with the new personality, which through accurate knowledge is being made new according to the image of the One who created it." (Col. 3:5-10) "This, therefore, I say and bear witness to in the Lord, that you no longer go on walking just as the nations also walk in the unprofitableness of their minds, while they are in darkness mentally, and alienated from the life that belongs to God, because of the ignorance that is in them, because of the insensibility of their hearts. Having come to be past all moral sense, they gave themselves over to loose conduct to work uncleanness of every sort with greediness. But you did not learn the Christ to be so, provided, indeed, that you heard him and were taught by means of him, just as truth is in Jesus, that you should put away the old personality which conforms to your former course of conduct and which is being corrupted according to his deceptive desires; but that you should be made new in the force actuating your mind, and should put on the new personality which was created according to God's will in true righteousness and loyalty." (Eph. 4:17-24)

Why is moral cleanness of all persons among Jehovah's people important to every one of us?

"Many will follow their acts of loose conduct, and on account of these the way of the truth will be spoken of abusively." (2 Pet. 2:2) "Beloved ones, though I was making every effort to write you about the salvation we hold in common, I found it necessary to write you to exhort you to put up a hard fight for the faith that was once for all time delivered to the holy ones. My reason is that certain men have slipped in who have long ago been appointed by the Scriptures to this judgment, ungodly men, turning the undeserved kindness of our God into an excuse for loose conduct and proving false to our only Owner and Lord, Jesus Christ." (Jude 3, 4; see also Joshua 7:1-26.)

When difficulties arise between individuals because of serious wrongs, what is the Christian way to handle the situation?

"If your brother commits a sin, go lay bare his fault between you and him alone. If he listens to you, you have gained your brother. But if he does not listen, take along with you one or two more, in order that at the mouth of two or three witnesses every matter may be established. If he does not listen to them, speak to the congregation. If he does not listen even to the congregation, let him be to you just as a man of the nations and as a tax collector." (Matt. 18:15-17)

What action does the congregation take when a person in its midst proves to be a persistent and unrepentant violator of God's commandments?

"In my letter I wrote you to quit mixing in company with fornicators, not meaning entirely with the fornicators of this world or the greedy persons and extortioners or idolaters. Otherwise, you would actually have to get out of the world. But now I am writing you to quit mixing in company with anyone called a brother that is a fornicator or a greedy person or an idolater or a reviler or a drunkard or an extortioner, not even eating with such a man. For what do I have to do with judging those outside? Do you not judge those inside, while God judges those outside? 'Remove the wicked man from among yourselves.'" (1 Cor. 5:9-13)

If a person in weakness commits a serious sin, but he wants help to be restored to Jehovah's favor, what action should he take?

"He that is covering over his transgressions will not succeed, but he that is confessing and leaving them will be shown mercy." (Prov. 28:13) "My sin I finally confessed to you, and my error I did not cover. I said: 'I shall make confession over my transgressions to Jehovah.' And you yourself pardoned the error of my sins." (Ps. 32:5) "My little children, I am writing you these things that you may not commit a sin. And yet, if anyone does commit a sin, we have a helper with the Father, Jesus Christ, a righteous one. And he is a propitiatory sacrifice for our sins, yet not for ours only but also for the whole world's." (1 John 2:1, 2) "Brothers, even though a man takes some false step before he is aware of it, you who have spiritual qualifications try to readjust such a man in a spirit of mildness, as you each keep an eye on yourself, for fear you also may be tempted." (Gal. 6:1) "Let him call the older men of the congregation to him, and let them pray over him, greasing him with oil in the name of Jehovah. And the prayer of faith will make the indisposed one well, and Jehovah will raise him up. Also, if he has committed sins, it will be forgiven him." (Jas. 5:14, 15)

What is the proper viewpoint to have when one is Scripturally reproved?

"The discipline of Jehovah, O my son, do not reject; and do not abhor his reproof, because the one whom Jehovah loves he reproves, even as a father does a son in whom he finds pleasure." (Prov. 3:11, 12) "The reproofs of discipline are the way of life." (Prov. 6:23) "Anyone shunning discipline is rejecting his own soul, but the one listening to reproof is acquiring heart." (Prov. 15:32) "All those for whom I [Jesus Christ] have affection I reprove and discipline. Therefore be zealous and repent." (Rev. 3:19) (See also Hebrews 12:5-11.)

What is the fruitage of the spirit, and is it reasonable to expect a Christian to manifest this fruitage in his life?

"Keep walking by spirit and you will carry out no fleshly desire at all. . . . The fruitage of the spirit is love, joy, peace, long-suffering, kindness, goodness, faith, mildness, self-control. . . . If we are living by spirit, let us go on walking orderly also by spirit." (Gal. 5:16, 22, 23, 25)

How should Christians view the shortcomings of fellow believers?

"Stop judging that you may not be judged; for with what judgment you are judging, you will be judged; and with the measure that you are measuring out, they will measure out to you. Why, then, do you look at the straw in your brother's eye, but do not consider the rafter in your own eye? Or how can you say to your brother, 'Allow me to extract the straw from your eye'; when, look! a rafter is in your own eye? Hypocrite! First extract the rafter from your own eye, and then you will see clearly how to extract the straw from your brother's eye." (Matt. 7:1-5) "The one covering over transgression is seeking love, and he that keeps talking about a matter is separating those familiar with one another." (Prov. 17:9) "The insight of a man certainly slows down his anger, and it is beauty on his part to pass over transgression." (Prov. 19:11)

What does the Bible say about sharing with other religious groups in worship or any of the other activities in which they engage?

"Do not become unevenly yoked with unbelievers. For what fellowship do righteousness and lawlessness have? Or what sharing does light have with darkness? Further, what harmony is there between Christ and Belial? Or what portion does a faithful person have with an unbeliever? And what agreement does God's temple have with idols? For we are a temple of a living God; just as God said: 'I shall reside among them and walk among them, and I shall be their God, and they will be my people.' ' "Therefore get out from among them, and separate yourselves," says Jehovah, "and quit touching the unclean thing" '; ' "and I will take you in." ' ' "And I shall be a father to you, and you will be sons and daughters to me," says Jehovah the Almighty.' " (2 Cor. 6:14-18) "I heard another voice out of heaven say: 'Get out of her, my people, if you do not want to share with her in her sins, and if you do not want to receive part of her plagues. For her sins have massed together clear up to heaven, and God has called her acts of injustice to mind.' " (Rev. 18:4, 5) "The things which the nations sacrifice they sacrifice to demons, and not to God; and I do not want you to become sharers with the demons." (1 Cor. 10:20) "Go in through the narrow gate; because broad and spacious is the road leading off into destruction, and many are the ones going in through it; whereas narrow is the gate and cramped the road leading off into life, and few are the ones finding it. Not everyone saying to me, 'Lord, Lord,' will enter into the kingdom of the heavens, but the one doing the will of my Father who is in the heavens will. Many will say to me in that day, 'Lord, Lord, did we not prophesy in your name, and expel demons in your name, and perform many powerful works in your name?' And yet then I will confess to them: I never knew you! Get away from me, you workers of lawlessness." (Matt. 7:13, 14, 21-23) "Men will be . . . having a form of godly devotion but proving false to its power; and from these turn away." (2 Tim. 3:2, 5) [Consider changes that this may necessitate in one's life.]

What is the only religious celebration that Christians are commanded to observe?

"I received from the Lord that which I also handed on to you, that the Lord Jesus in the night in which he was going to be handed over took a loaf and, after giving thanks, he broke it and said: 'This means my body which is in your behalf. Keep doing this in remembrance of me.' He did likewise respecting the cup also, after he had the evening meal, saying: 'This cup means the new covenant by virtue of my blood. Keep doing this, as often as you drink it, in remembrance of me.' For as often as you eat this loaf and drink this cup, you keep proclaiming the death of the Lord, until he arrives." (1 Cor. 11:23-26)

What Bible principles should guide us in determining whether other celebrations that are popular in the community are acceptable for Christians?

"They are no part of the world, just as I am no part of the world." (John 17:16) "Do not be loving either the world or the things in the world. If anyone loves the world, the love of the Father is not in him; because everything in the world—the desire of the flesh and the desire of the eyes and the showy display of one's means of life—does not originate with the Father, but originates with the world. Furthermore, the world is passing away and so is its desire, but he that does the will of God remains forever." (1 John 2:15-17) "When Herod's birthday was being celebrated the daughter of Herodias danced at it and pleased Herod so much that he promised with an oath to give her whatever she asked. Then she, under her mother's coaching, said: 'Give me here upon a platter the head of John the Baptist.' Grieved though he was, the king out of regard for his oaths and for those reclining with him commanded it to be given; and he sent and had John beheaded in the prison." (Matt. 14:6-10) "The time that has passed by is sufficient for you to have worked out the will of the nations when you proceeded in deeds of loose conduct, lusts, excesses with wine, revelries, drinking matches, and illegal idolatries." (1 Pet. 4:3) "What fellowship do righteousness and lawlessness have? Or what sharing does light have with darkness? Further, what harmony is there between Christ and Belial? Or what portion does a faithful person have with an unbeliever? And what agreement does God's temple have with idols? . . . ' "Therefore get out from among them, and separate yourselves," says Jehovah, "and quit touching the unclean thing" '; ' "and I will take you in." ' " (2 Cor. 6:14-17) [Analyze application of these scriptures to activities that are popular in your area.]

Whom does the Bible identify as the "ruler of the world" and "the god of this system of things"?

"I shall not speak much with you anymore, for the ruler of the world is coming. And he has no hold on me [Jesus Christ]." (John 14:30) "We know we originate with God, but the whole world is lying in the power of the wicked one." (1 John 5:19) "The god of this system of things has blinded the minds of the unbelievers, that the illumination of the glorious good news about the Christ, who is the image of God, might not shine through." (2 Cor. 4:4) "Down the great dragon was hurled, the original serpent, the one called Devil and Satan, who is misleading the entire inhabited earth; he was hurled down to the earth, and his angels were hurled down with him." (Rev. 12:9)

What is the position of Christians as to this world alienated from God?

"If you were part of the world, the world would be fond of what is its own. Now because you are no part of the world, but I have chosen you out of the world, on this account the world hates you." (John 15:19) "Do you not know that the friendship with the world is enmity with God? Whoever, therefore, wants to be a friend of the world is constituting himself an enemy of God." (Jas. 4:4)

What was Jesus' attitude toward all participation in the political affairs of the world?

"The Devil took him along to an unusually high mountain, and showed him all the kingdoms of the world and their glory, and he said to him: 'All these things I will give you if you fall down and do an act of worship to me.' Then Jesus said to him: 'Go away, Satan! For it is written, "It is Jehovah your God you must worship, and it is to him alone you must render sacred service."'" (Matt. 4:8-10) "Jesus, knowing they were about to come and seize him to make him king, withdrew again into the mountain all alone." (John 6:15) "Jesus answered: 'My kingdom is no part of this world. If my kingdom were part of this world, my attendants would have fought that I should not be delivered up to the Jews. But, as it is, my kingdom is not from this source.'" (John 18:36) [Consider the application of these texts to situations that arise in your locality.]

How do Bible commands concerning idolatry affect a Christian in this modern world?

"Guard yourselves from idols." (1 John 5:21) "You must not make for yourself a carved image or a form like anything that is in the heavens above or that is on the earth underneath or that is in the waters under the earth. You must not bow down to them nor be induced to serve them, because I Jehovah your God am a God exacting exclusive devotion." (Ex. 20:4, 5) "I am Jehovah. That is my name; and to no one else shall I give my own glory, neither my praise to graven images." (Isa. 42:8) "Their idols are silver and gold, the work of the hands of earthling man. A mouth they have, but they cannot speak; eyes they have, but they cannot see; ears they have, but they cannot hear. A nose they have, but they cannot smell. Hands are theirs, but they cannot feel. Feet are theirs, but they cannot walk; they utter no sound with their throat. Those making them will become just like them, all those who are trusting in them." (Ps. 115:4-8) "Nebuchadnezzar the king made an image of gold, the height of which was sixty cubits and the breadth of which was six cubits. He set it up in the plain of Dura in the jurisdictional district of Babylon. . . . And the herald was crying out loudly: 'To you it is being said, O peoples, national groups and languages, . . . fall down and worship the image of gold that Nebuchadnezzar the king has set up. And whoever does not fall down and worship will at the same moment be thrown into the burning fiery furnace.' . . . Shadrach, Meshach and Abednego answered, and they were saying to the king: . . . 'let it become known to you, O king, that your gods are not the ones we are serving, and the image of gold that you have set up we will not worship.'" (Dan. 3:1-18) "On a set day Herod clothed himself with royal raiment and sat down upon the judgment seat and began giving them a public address. In turn the assembled people began shouting: 'A god's voice, and not a man's!' Instantly the angel of Jehovah struck him, because he did not give the glory to God; and he became eaten up with worms and expired." (Acts 12:21-23) "If anyone worships the wild beast and its image, and receives a mark on his forehead or upon his hand, he will also drink of the wine of the anger of God that is poured out undiluted into the cup of his wrath, and he shall be tormented with fire and sulphur in the sight of the holy angels and in the sight of the Lamb. And the smoke of their torment ascends forever and ever, and day and night they have no rest, those who worship the wild beast and its image, and whoever receives the mark of its name. Here is where it means endurance for the holy ones, those who observe the commandments of God and the faith of Jesus." (Rev. 14:9-12) [Give examples of situations calling for application of this counsel.]

In the light of the following texts, what is the position of a true Christian in this world?

"It must occur in the final part of the days that the mountain of the house of Jehovah will become firmly established above the top of the mountains, and it will certainly be lifted up above the hills; and to it all the nations must stream. And many peoples will certainly go and say: 'Come, you people, and let us go up to the mountain of Jehovah, to the house of the God of Jacob; and he will instruct us about his ways, and we will walk in his paths.' For out of Zion law will go forth, and the word of Jehovah out of Jerusalem. And he will certainly render judgment among the nations and set matters straight respecting many peoples. And they will have to beat their swords into plowshares and their spears into pruning shears. Nation will not lift up sword against nation, neither will they learn war anymore." (Isa. 2:2-4) "They are no part of the world, just as I am no part of the world." (John 17:16) "Do not you people be owing anybody a single thing, except to love one another; for he that loves his fellowman has fulfilled the law. For the law code, 'You must not commit adultery, You must not murder, You must not steal, You must not covet,' and whatever other commandment there is, is summed up in this word, namely, 'You must love your neighbor as yourself.' Love does not work evil to one's neighbor; therefore love is the law's fulfillment." (Rom. 13:8-10) "You were bought with a price; stop becoming slaves of men." (1 Cor. 7:23)

Is it necessary for a Christian to be subject to worldly rulers and to show them respect?

"Let every soul be in subjection to the superior authorities, for there is no authority except by God; the existing authorities stand placed in their relative positions by God. Therefore he who opposes the authority has taken a stand against the arrangement of God; those who have taken a stand against it will receive judgment to themselves. For those ruling are an object of fear, not to the good deed, but to the bad. Do you, then, want to have no fear of the authority? Keep doing good, and you will have praise from it; for it is God's minister to you for your good. But if you are doing what is bad, be in fear: for it is not without purpose that it bears the sword; for it is God's minister, an avenger to express wrath upon the one practicing what is bad. There is therefore compelling reason for you people to be in subjection, not only on account of that wrath but also on account of your conscience. For that is why you are also paying taxes; for they are God's public servants constantly serving this very purpose." (Rom. 13:1-6) "Continue reminding them to be in subjection and be obedient to governments and authorities as rulers, to be ready for every good work." (Titus 3:1) "Concerning all the things of which I am accused by Jews, King Agrippa, I count myself happy that it is before you I am to make my defense this day, especially as you are expert on all the customs as well as the controversies among Jews. Therefore I beg you to hear me patiently." (Acts 26:2, 3)

Must a Christian pay all the taxes demanded by law?

"They questioned him, saying: 'Teacher, we know you speak and teach correctly and show no partiality, but you teach the way of God in line with truth: Is it lawful for us to pay tax to Caesar or not?' But he detected their cunning and said to them: 'Show me a denarius. Whose image and inscription does it have?' They said: 'Caesar's.' He said to them: 'By all means, then, pay back Caesar's things to Caesar, but God's things to God.'" (Luke 20:21-25) "Render to all their dues, to him who calls for the tax, the tax; to him who calls for the tribute, the tribute; to him who calls for fear, such fear; to him who calls for honor, such honor." (Rom. 13:7)

Is there any circumstance under which a Christian would not obey the law?

"We wish to conduct ourselves honestly in all things." (Heb. 13:18) "Hold a good conscience, so that in the particular in which you are spoken against they may get ashamed who are speaking slightingly of your good conduct in connection with Christ. For it is better to suffer because you are doing good, if the will of God wishes it, than because you are doing evil." (1 Pet. 3:16, 17) "They called them and charged them, nowhere to make any utterance or to teach upon the basis of the name of Jesus. But in reply Peter and John said to them: 'Whether it is righteous in the sight of God to listen to you rather than to God, judge for yourselves. But as for us, we cannot stop speaking about the things we have seen and heard.'" (Acts 4:18-20) "'We positively ordered you not to keep teaching upon the basis of this name, and yet, look! you have filled Jerusalem with your teaching, and you are determined to bring the blood of this man upon us.' In answer Peter and the other apostles said: 'We must obey God as ruler rather than men.'" (Acts 5:28, 29)

Why are true Christians persecuted?

"If you were part of the world, the world would be fond of what is its own. Now because you are no part of the world, but I have chosen you out of the world, on this account the world hates you. Bear in mind the word I said to you, A slave is not greater than his master. If they have persecuted me, they will persecute you also; if they have observed my word, they will observe yours also. But they will do all these things against you on account of my name, because they do not know him that sent me." (John 15:19-21) "In fact, all those desiring to live with godly devotion in association with Christ Jesus will also be persecuted." (2 Tim. 3:12) "Before all these things people will lay their hands upon you and persecute you, delivering you up to the synagogues and prisons, you being haled before kings and governors for the sake of my name. It will turn out to you for a witness." (Luke 21:12, 13)

What are some factors to consider in determining whether certain types of employment are proper for Christians?

"Let the stealer steal no more, but rather let him do hard work, doing with his hands what is good work, that he may have something to distribute to someone in need." (Eph. 4:28) "The Devil . . . is a liar and the father of the lie." (John 8:44) "I heard another voice out of heaven say: 'Get out of her [Babylon the Great], my people, if you do not want to share with her in her sins, and if you do not want to receive part of her

plagues.' " (Rev. 18:4) "What! Do you not know that
unrighteous persons will not inherit God's kingdom? Do
not be misled. Neither fornicators, nor idolaters, nor
adulterers, nor men kept for unnatural purposes, nor
men who lie with men, nor thieves, nor greedy persons,
nor drunkards, nor revilers, nor extortioners will inherit God's kingdom. And yet that is what some of you
were. But you have been washed clean, but you have
been sanctified, but you have been declared righteous in
the name of our Lord Jesus Christ and with the spirit of
our God." (1 Cor. 6:9-11) " 'Come, you people, and let
us go up to the mountain of Jehovah and to the house
of the God of Jacob; and he will instruct us about his
ways, and we will walk in his paths.' For out of Zion
law will go forth, and the word of Jehovah out of Jerusalem. And he will certainly render judgment among
many peoples, and set matters straight respecting
mighty nations far away. And they will have to beat
their swords into plowshares and their spears into pruning shears. They will not lift up sword, nation against
nation, neither will they learn war anymore." (Mic.
4:2, 3) "Write them to abstain . . . from blood." (Acts
15:20) "Jesus, knowing they were about to come and
seize him to make him king, withdrew again into the
mountain all alone." (John 6:15)

What should always be our attitude toward the doing of Jehovah's will?

"Look! I am come to do your will." (Heb. 10:9) "Happy is the man in fear of Jehovah, in whose commandments he has taken very much delight." (Ps. 112:1)
"You must love Jehovah your God with your whole
heart and with your whole soul and with your whole
strength and with your whole mind." (Luke 10:27) "Jesus said to them: 'My food is for me to do the will of
him that sent me and to finish his work.' " (John 4:34)

Why are Christians called Jehovah's witnesses?

" 'You are my witnesses,' is the utterance of Jehovah,
'even my servant whom I have chosen, in order that you
may know and have faith in me, and that you may understand that I am the same One. Before me there was
no God formed, and after me there continued to be none.
I—I am Jehovah, and besides me there is no savior. I
myself have told forth and have saved and have caused

it to be heard, when there was among you no strange
god. So you are my witnesses,' is the utterance of Jehovah, 'and I am God.' " (Isa. 43:10-12) "Jesus Christ, 'the
Faithful Witness,' 'The firstborn from the dead,' and
'The Ruler of the kings of the earth.' " (Rev. 1:5)

Who or what is the "faithful and discreet slave"?

" 'Have no fear, *little flock*, because your Father has
approved of giving you the kingdom. Let your loins be
girded and your lamps be burning, and you yourselves
be like men waiting for their master when he returns
from the marriage, so that at his arriving and knocking
they may at once open to him. Happy are those slaves
whom the master on arriving finds watching! . . . You
also, keep ready, because at an hour that you do not
think likely the Son of man is coming.' Then Peter
said: 'Lord, are you saying this illustration to us or
also to all?' And the Lord said: 'Who really is the faithful steward, the discreet one, whom his master will appoint over his body of attendants to keep giving them
their measure of food supplies at the proper time? Happy is that slave, if his master on arriving finds him
doing so! I tell you truthfully, He will appoint him
over all his belongings.' " (Luke 12:32, 35-44; see also
Matthew 24:45-47.) "You are my witnesses, . . . my servant." (Isa. 43:10)

What is the governing body of the Christian congregation, and what purpose does it serve?

" 'Brothers, search out for yourselves seven certified
men from among you, full of spirit and wisdom, that
we may appoint them over this necessary business' . . .
and they placed them before the apostles, and, after
having prayed, these laid their hands upon them."
(Acts 6:1-6) "When the apostles in Jerusalem heard
that Samaria had accepted the word of God, they
dispatched Peter and John to them." (Acts 8:14) "Certain men . . . began to teach the brothers: 'Unless you
get circumcised according to the custom of Moses, you
cannot be saved.' But when there had occurred no
little dissension and disputing by Paul and Barnabas
with them, they arranged for Paul and Barnabas and
some others of them to go up to the apostles and
older men in Jerusalem regarding this dispute. . . .

And the apostles and the older men gathered together to see about this affair." (Acts 15:1-29)

What attitude should Christians show toward those who serve as shepherds in the congregation?

"Now we request you, brothers, to have regard for those who are working hard among you and presiding over you in the Lord and admonishing you; and to give them more than extraordinary consideration in love because of their work." (1 Thess. 5:12, 13) "Be obedient to those who are taking the lead among you and be submissive, for they are keeping watch over your souls as those who will render an account; that they may do this with joy and not with sighing, for this would be damaging to you." (Heb. 13:17)

Why is it beneficial to attend the meetings arranged by the congregation?

"Let us consider one another to incite to love and fine works, not forsaking the gathering of ourselves together, as some have the custom, but encouraging one another, and all the more so as you behold the day drawing near." (Heb. 10:24, 25) "One isolating himself will seek his own selfish longing; against all practical wisdom he will break forth." (Prov. 18:1) "I am longing to see you, . . . that there may be an interchange of encouragement among you, by each one through the other's faith, both yours and mine." (Rom. 1:11, 12)

Why is personal study important in the life of a Christian?

"Now the latter were more noble-minded than those in Thessalonica, for they received the word with the greatest eagerness of mind, carefully examining the Scriptures daily as to whether these things were so." (Acts 17:11) "This book of the law should not depart from your mouth, and you must in an undertone read in it day and night, in order that you may take care to do according to all that is written in it; for then you will make your way successful and then you will act wisely." (Josh. 1:8) "Ponder over these things; be absorbed in them, that your advancement may be manifest to all persons." (1 Tim. 4:15)

What urgent work does the Bible set out for all Christians at this time?

"This good news of the kingdom will be preached in all the inhabited earth for a witness to all the nations; and then the end will come." (Matt. 24:14) "All authority has been given me in heaven and on the earth. Go therefore and make disciples of people of all the nations, baptizing them in the name of the Father and of the Son and of the holy spirit, teaching them to observe all the things I have commanded you. And, look! I am with you all the days until the conclusion of the system of things." (Matt. 28:18-20)

In what various ways may this work be accomplished?

"He went journeying from city to city and from village to village, preaching and declaring the good news of the kingdom of God." (Luke 8:1) "A certain woman named Martha received him as guest into the house. This woman also had a sister called Mary, who, however, sat down at the feet of the Lord and kept listening to his word." (Luke 10:38, 39) "Now Jesus, tired out from the journey, was sitting at the fountain just as he was. The hour was about the sixth. A woman of Samaria came to draw water. . . . Jesus said to her: 'Everyone drinking from this water will get thirsty again. Whoever drinks from the water that I will give him will never get thirsty at all, but the water that I will give him will become in him a fountain of water bubbling up to impart everlasting life.' The woman said to him: 'Sir, give me this water, so that I may neither thirst nor keep coming over to this place to draw water.' " (John 4:6-15) "According to Paul's custom . . . he reasoned with them from the Scriptures. Consequently he began to reason in the synagogue with the Jews and the other people who worshiped God and every day in the marketplace with those who happened to be on hand." (Acts 17:2, 17) "I did not hold back from telling you any of the things that were profitable nor from teaching you publicly and from house to house." (Acts 20:20)

Is this work done in our own strength?

"We have this treasure in earthen vessels, that the power beyond what is normal may be God's and not that out of ourselves." (2 Cor. 4:7) "The Lord stood near me and infused power into me, that through me the preaching might be fully accomplished and all the nations might hear it." (2 Tim. 4:17) "I saw another angel flying in midheaven, and he had everlasting good news to declare as glad tidings to those who dwell on the earth, and to every nation and tribe and tongue and people." (Rev. 14:6)

Why should one who has sincerely repented and turned around and chosen to be a disciple of Christ be baptized?

"Go therefore and make disciples of people of all the nations, baptizing them in the name of the Father and of the Son and of the holy spirit." (Matt. 28:19) "Then Jesus came from Galilee to the Jordan to John, in order to be baptized by him. But the latter tried to prevent him, saying: 'I am the one needing to be baptized by you, and are you coming to me?' In reply Jesus said to him: 'Let it be, this time, for in that way it is suitable for us to carry out all that is righteous.' Then he quit preventing him. After being baptized Jesus immediately came up from the water; and, look! the heavens were opened up, and he saw descending like a dove God's spirit coming upon him. Look! Also, there was a voice from the heavens that said: 'This is my Son, the beloved, whom I have approved.'" (Matt. 3: 13-17) "When they believed Philip, who was declaring the good news of the kingdom of God and of the name of Jesus Christ, they proceeded to be baptized, both men and women." (Acts 8:12) "Philip opened his mouth and . . . declared to him the good news about Jesus. Now as they were going over the road, they came to a certain body of water, and the eunuch said: 'Look! A body of water; what prevents me from getting baptized?'" (Acts 8:35, 36) "On hearing this, they got baptized in the name of the Lord Jesus." (Acts 19:5) "And now why are you delaying? Rise, get baptized and wash your sins away by your calling upon his name." (Acts 22:16) "That which corresponds to this is also now saving you, namely, baptism, (not the putting away of the filth of the flesh, but the request made to God for a good conscience,) through the resurrection of Jesus Christ." (1 Pet. 3:21)

CHAPTER 4

SHEPHERDS OF THE FLOCK OF GOD

WITH appealing warmth, the Bible describes the way that Jehovah deals with his people, saying: "Look! The Sovereign Lord Jehovah himself will come even as a strong one . . . Like a shepherd he will shepherd his own drove. With his arm he will collect together the lambs; and in his bosom he will carry them. Those giving suck he will conduct with care." (Isa. 40:10, 11) He is the "shepherd and overseer" of our souls. And he has made his Son the "chief shepherd" of his flock. (1 Pet. 2:25; 5:4) Loving provisions have been made to care for that flock.

After Jesus left the earth and returned to the heavenly presence of his Father, he gave "gifts in men" to the Christian congregation. "He gave some as apostles, some as prophets, some as evangelizers, some as shepherds and teachers, with a view to the readjustment of the holy ones, for ministerial work, for the building up of the body of the Christ." (Eph. 4:8, 11, 12) At the start the apostles evidently took the lead in these activities, publicly declaring the good news and then shepherding and teaching those who became believers.—Acts 2:42; 5:40-42.

With an increase in the number of believers, new congregations developed, and in each of them "older men" were appointed to provide needed supervision, the kind of supervision that a shepherd gives to sheep. (Acts 14:23) But the "flock" did not belong to them. As the apostle Paul reminded overseers in the congregation of Ephesus, they were shepherds of "the congregation *of God,* which he purchased with the blood of his own Son." (Acts 20:28) And when pointing out the responsibility of "older men" in relation to the congregation, Peter wrote: "Shepherd the flock *of God* in your care." (1 Pet. 5:1, 2) So, as shepherds, they were to help the congregation to appreciate and maintain its proper relationship to God and his Son.

It is noteworthy that the Bible does not say that there was only one "older man," one overseer, in each congregation. Rather, it indicates that there were a number of such. (Acts 20:17, 28; Phil. 1:1) What was their relationship to the other members of the "flock of God"?

ELDERS, OVERSEERS, SHEPHERDS

Their designations help to make their position evident. They were to be "older men" or "elders," "overseers" and "shepherds." The term "older men" or "elders" tells us something about their qualities as well as indicating their position within the congregation. Being an older man in the literal sense is associated with having experience in dealing with life's problems, hence with wisdom and judgment. (Compare Job 32:6, 7.) So, in a spiritual sense these brothers were to be like the older men or elders of a community to whom people could look for sound counsel and guidance, and to whom problems could be brought for advice or judgment.

The term "overseer" describes their work on behalf of the congregation. In the original Greek a basic thought conveyed by this term (e·pi'sko·pos) is that of 'protective care and supervision' by one who visits and inspects. But this overseeing does not make them superior to their brothers. Jesus was very definite about this, saying to his apostles: "You know that the rulers of the nations lord it over them and the great men wield authority over them. This is not the way among you; but whoever wants to become great among you must be your minister, and whoever wants to be first among you must be your slave." (Matt. 20:25-27) Though taking the lead in ministering, they would not assume the title of "leader," for Christ Jesus was their one Leader. (Matt. 23:8-11; Heb. 13:7, 17, 24) They would take the lead especially by becoming "examples to the flock." But never would it be in keeping with their position for them to act as if they owned the flock or to look upon the brothers as their servants; the flock is "God's inheritance" and he has given it to "our only Owner and Lord, Jesus Christ." (1 Pet. 5:3; Jude 4) As Paul wrote: "Not that we are the masters over your faith, but we are *fellow workers* for your joy, for it is by your faith that you are standing." —2 Cor. 1:24.

So their overseeing is well described by the further

designation "shepherd." A shepherd is assigned by the owner of a flock to guide it into well-watered and good pasture, to protect it from attack and harm, to keep the sheep from straying, and to go out and look for those that do stray or get lost. He must also care for sick or lame sheep, dressing their wounds and applying healing applications, and he needs to be careful not to set too fast a pace for those with young lambs. (Compare Psalm 23; Genesis 33:13; 1 Samuel 17:33-36.) To do this in a spiritual way for the congregation would mean hard work for the shepherds, but they were to do it "willingly" and "eagerly." (1 Pet. 5:1, 2; Acts 20:28-35) It would be a heavy responsibility, for they would be keeping watch over the souls of God's "sheep" and would themselves have to "render an account" to their Owner. They should want to be able to give a good report of their shepherding, as did God's Son at the end of his earthly course.—Heb. 13:17; John 17:6, 12.

WHAT IS INCLUDED

When the Lord Jesus spoke to Peter about 'shepherding,' he drew attention to one of the principal duties involved, saying: "Feed my little sheep." (John 21:15-17) Just as the "sheep" are figurative, so is the 'food.' The nourishment is drawn from the Word of God. (Matt. 4:4; 1 Tim. 4:6) And it is the responsibility of all who are shepherds to aid the congregation to gain that nourishment, doing so by teaching. The apostle Paul associates shepherding with teaching, saying that Christ gave to his congregation "some as shepherds and teachers." (Eph. 4:8, 11) Much of their teaching is done in the meetings of the congregation, over which they should preside.

Of himself as the "fine shepherd," Jesus said: "I know my sheep and my sheep know me." (John 10:14) Those who, as shepherds, seek to imitate Jesus also need to know well the "flock of God" entrusted to their care. They can show their concern for each one by speaking to them personally at the congregation meetings, also accompanying them in the field ministry.

However, since the Greek term for 'exercising oversight' (e·pi·sko·pe'o) includes the meaning of 'visiting,' it is certainly appropriate that the shepherds visit the brothers in their homes and even in prison, upbuilding them and contributing to their spiritual enlightenment. (Compare Revelation 3:20; Luke 10:38-42; Matthew 25:36, 39.) Paul reminded the elders of Ephesus that he had taught them, not only publicly, but also "from house to house."* (Acts 20:17-20, margin; *Mo; RS; Lamsa; Yg; Dy; Knox;* Acts 18:19-21; 19:1-19; 20:31) A congregation was established in Ephesus and other cities. For lack of public meeting places that could be rented or hired, the local congregation would meet in the private home of a dedicated, baptized believer (Rom. 16:5; Col. 4:15; Philem. 2), and to congregational meetings interested persons could be invited. By these means the members of the congregation would come to know the overseers well and feel free to approach them, and the overseers, in turn, would become better acquainted with the needs of each one of the "flock." It is important for overseers to be approachable, willing to listen when their brothers come to them with problems, and dealing with them in a manner that will result in refreshment, as the "fine shepherd" set the example.—Matt. 11:28-30.

---

* A similar work "from house to house" is referred to in Acts 5:42. Here some modern translators (*RS; Mo; NA*) render the Greek expression here (*kat' oi'kon*) as "at home." On this we refer to a comment made by Dr. A. T. Robertson, the author of the 1454-page book *A Grammar of the Greek New Testament in the Light of Historical Research* (1934). Referring to such a rendering, he says in his book *Word Pictures in the New Testament,* Volume III on "The Acts of the Apostles," page 70, paragraph 3:

"*In the temple and at home (en toi hieroi kai kat' oikon).* This was a distinct triumph to go back to the temple where they had been arrested (verse 25) and at home or from house to house, as it probably means (chapter 2:46). It was a great day for the disciples in Jerusalem."

As regards the translation "from house to house" (*kat' oi'kous*) in Acts 20:20, which some modern translators would render as: "at your houses" (*AT*), "in your homes" (*Je; NE*), "in private" (*NA*), Doctor Robertson has this to say on pages 349, 350, paragraph 1:

"*and from house to house (kai kat' oikous).* By (according to) houses. It is worth noting that this greatest of preachers preached from house to house and did not make his visits merely social calls. He was doing kingdom business all the while as in the house of Aquila and Priscilla (1 Cor. 16:19)."

On page 107 of *A Manual Grammar of the Greek New Testament,* by Dana and Mantey (1927), we read concerning the Greek preposition *kata'* and its meanings according to the cases of the nouns that follow it: "114. Root meaning: *down.* In composition: *down.* . . . Also in the distributive sense: Acts 2:46, *kat' oikon, from house to house;* Luke 2:41, *kat' etos, from year to year;* 1 Cor. 14:27, *kata duo, by twos;* see also Luke 8:1; 13:32."

The overseers are, of course, interested in the work being done by their brothers and sisters in Kingdom-preaching and in the making of disciples. They appreciate the importance of this work in the accomplishment of God's purpose. They also realize that one's participation in this activity reflects appreciation of Jehovah, of his Son and of the issue that the Devil raised over the rightness of Jehovah's sovereignty, as well as concern for one's fellowman. So, when speaking to their brothers as a congregation and privately, the overseers endeavor to stimulate appreciation for this grand privilege of service.—Rom. 10:13, 14; Heb. 13:15.

But our walking in the way of the truth involves far more than preaching to others. When Paul wrote to Titus, an overseer in Crete, about the things concerning which to 'exhort' his Christian brothers, he emphasized their being "zealous for fine works." As the context shows, those "fine works" involve all of a Christian's activities, including his homelife, his secular work, and his obedience to law. (Titus 2:1–3:8) Titus was to speak about these matters, but, of course, he was not to intrude needlessly in the private affairs of others. And when offering counsel he was to 'hold firmly to the faithful word,' that is, to God's own Word.—Titus 1:9.

While encouraging his brothers to be "zealous for fine works," there is nothing in the Scriptures to suggest that an overseer is to try to force service from his brothers. Each Christian is to bear the spiritual yoke of discipleship as unto God and Christ, not unto men. (Matt. 11:29, 30; Rom. 14:4; Col. 3:23, 24) Any "rod" of authority granted the overseers is to be used, not to prod the "sheep" to greater speed, but to protect and rescue, or, where necessary, to correct and reprove. The Oriental shepherd equipped with rod and staff went ahead of the flock of sheep as the one taking the lead and setting the pace for the flock. (John 10:4; Ps. 23:4; 2 Cor. 13:10; 1 Cor. 4:21) Thus, the overseers would encourage the brothers to feed their minds and hearts regularly on God's Word (Ps. 1:2; Phil. 1:9, 10), to share fully in the preaching of the good news (Mark 13:10; 1 Cor. 9:16), to be hospitable to one another (Rom. 12:13; Heb. 13:2), and to abound in similar fine works. But they would not try to make rules as to how much each one should do and when and how. Rather, their desire would be to cultivate appreciation, so that the individual would respond "willingly" and out of love.—Ps. 110:3; 1 Cor. 13:3.

Of course, situations may arise in which members of the congregation deviate from Christian ways, practicing what is wrong, and then it is the responsibility of the overseers to correct, reprove and reprimand, preferably with mildness, but with severity where necessary. (2 Tim. 2:24-26; 4:2; 1 Tim. 5:20; Titus 1:5, 13) They should deal with their spiritual brothers and sisters as they would their own fathers, mothers, brothers and sisters, or children. (1 Tim. 5:1, 2) Their aim should be, not to hurt by cutting speech, but to guide straying "sheep" back into the path of life and to protect the flock against any wolfish elements that might do injury to them. (Rom. 12:17-19; Matt. 18:12-14; Acts 20:28-30) If their way of dealing with the congregation shows loving concern for the "flock," they will surely gain the respect, love and cooperation of their brothers. —1 Thess. 2:7, 8, 11; 5:12-15.

It readily becomes apparent that there is much work for the elders in a congregation to do. To care for it properly, they may need assistance, and the Bible makes provision for that. In the introduction of his letter to the Philippians, when Paul mentions e·pi'sko·poi or "overseers," he also refers to di·a'ko·noi or "ministerial servants." The term di·a'ko·noi refers to those who are in the service of others, or attendants. The way in which Paul used the term indicates that these men had something to do with congregation arrangement. They were men ministering to the congregation by caring mainly for necessary nonshepherding matters, thus enabling the overseers to concentrate their time and attention on their teaching and other shepherding activity.—Compare Acts 6:1-6.

QUALIFYING TO BE ELDERS

How are elders put into office and thus entrusted with responsibility for shepherding the "flock"? The answer to this is indicated in the Bible book entitled "Acts of Apostles." There we learn that Paul had been chosen as an apostle by Jesus Christ, and he and Barnabas were sent out on a ministerial trip by instructions of God's holy spirit and with the laying on of hands of the responsible men of the congregation. (Acts 13:1-3) After preaching in certain cities, they later returned and strengthened the disciples. Additionally, Acts 14:23 relates: "They [that is, Paul and Barnabas] appointed older men for them in [each] congregation and, offering prayer with fastings, they committed them to Jehovah in whom they had become believers." Because this apostolic appointment of elders was accompanied by the laying on of hands (as indicated by the Greek verb used here) some modern translators prefer to use the word "ordained" instead of "appointed." (Acts 14: 23, *AV; Lamsa; Schonfield; Int*; vs. 22, *Dy*) So there was no popular election of elders in the congregations. Similarly, Timothy and Titus, as representatives of the Christian governing body, evidently made appointments of elders in harmony with instructions received from Paul.—1 Tim. 5:22; Titus 1:5.

The instructions that guided in the selection of elders or overseers back then are part of the inspired Word of God, and they continue to provide the basis for determining who qualify for appointment. Those instructions, as recorded at 1 Timothy 3:1-7, read:

"If any man is reaching out for an office of overseer, he is desirous of a fine work. The overseer should therefore be irreprehensible, a husband of one wife, moderate in habits, sound in mind, orderly, hospitable, qualified to teach, not a drunken brawler, not a smiter, but reasonable, not belligerent, not a lover of money, a man presiding over his own household in a fine manner, having children in subjection with all seriousness; (if indeed any man does not know how to preside over his own household, how will he take care of God's congregation?) not a newly converted man, for fear that he might get puffed up with pride and fall into the judgment passed upon the Devil. Moreover, he should also have a fine testimony from people on the outside, in order that he might not fall into reproach and a snare of the Devil."

A comparable list of qualifications for elders or overseers is found at Titus 1:5-9, but the language used, when compared with what is found at 1 Timothy 3:1-7, helps one to get a clearer view of what is involved.

The standards are not so high that they cannot be reached by any man in the congregation. But they do assure that the ones accredited as elders will be persons who are good examples in the congregation of God, not persons who may be outstanding because of 'worldly wisdom.' (1 Cor. 2:6, 7) What is looked for is evidence that one conscientiously applies the counsel of God's Word to all the affairs of life. He should be, not a mere boy nor a newly converted person, but a man who has had ample experience in Christian living. However, it is not mere physical age that qualifies one to be an elder in the congregation. He should have a broad knowledge of God's Word and a deep understanding of it, coupled with genuine love for the congregation, so that others will look to him with confidence when in need of counsel and will respect his judgment. (Job 32:9) He must also have the courage to speak up when there is wrongdoing, so that he will take any needed action to correct wrongdoing and to protect the "flock" against any who would selfishly exploit them. It is noteworthy that his being "qualified to teach" within the congregation, to exhort and to reprove are important factors in his being accredited as an elder.

After listing the requirements for those who would serve as overseers in the congregations, Paul also sets out the qualifications to be met by those designated as "ministerial servants." He says:

"Ministerial servants should likewise be serious, not double-tongued, not giving themselves to a lot of wine, not greedy of dishonest gain, holding the sacred secret of the faith with a clean conscience. Also, let these be tested as to fitness first, then let them serve as ministers, as they are free from accusation. Let ministerial servants be husbands of one wife, presiding in a fine manner over children and their own households. For the men who minister in a fine manner are acquiring for themselves a fine standing and great freeness of speech in the faith in connection with Christ Jesus." —1 Tim. 3:8-10, 12, 13.

These requirements, when compared with those for overseers, indicate that the ministerial servants' responsibility would involve work other than teaching and shepherding. Yet, the high standard set would serve to protect the congregation from any legitimate accusation as to the kind of men to whom it entrusted special responsibilities. They were not to be mere youths but "men," each one a fine example that would be viewed with respect by others. And they were to be persons who, over a sufficient period of time, had been "tested as to fitness," so that there would be assurance of their stability and dependability when entrusted with responsibility. Though their work differs from that of the elders, it is no less a part of their service to God and important to the smooth functioning of the congregation. In time, if they discharge their obligations well and also acquire the further qualifications needed by shepherds and teachers, they may be privileged to serve as elders in the congregation.

The Bible does not limit the number of elders or overseers that a congregation may have. They are mentioned in the plural number with regard to congregations at Jerusalem, Ephesus and Philippi. (Acts 21:15, 18; 20:17; Phil. 1:1) Doubtless this was true in all the congregations where there were more than one qualified brother. So Paul could rightly say: "If any man is reaching out for an office of overseer, he is desirous of a fine work." (1 Tim. 3:1) Such a privilege of service was open to any qualified brother who, because of love for Jehovah and for His "sheep," desired to share in the fine work of a Christian shepherd.

Appropriately, therefore, in each congregation of Jehovah's Christian witnesses, once a year, about September 1, those who are already appointed elders prayerfully consider whether any additional brothers who are active in service on behalf of the congregation now qualify to become elders. They also consider any who might now become ministerial servants. (If there are not at least three elders in the congregation, then the brothers serving as presiding overseer, field overseer and Bible study overseer make these recommendations, even though some of them are at the time serving only as substitutes.)

In making recommendations, the elders bear a serious responsibility before God to act in full harmony with his Word, not treating lightly any of the requirements that he has had recorded there. If there are some who now qualify for appointment, the body of elders makes a written recommendation to the governing body, sending it to the branch at its address in their country. With each name, they indicate the person's age, the date of his baptism, whether he professes to be of the "anointed" or of the "other sheep," and whether he is being recommended for appointment as an elder or as a ministerial servant and stating what his hitherto service position, if any, has been. This letter is signed by the presiding overseer, the field overseer and the Bible study overseer as representatives of the body of elders.

On receipt of the recommendations, the governing body through its appointed representatives makes the appointments. But this is not done according to some standard that they themselves set up. It is done in accord with what is set out in God's inspired Word, so it can truthfully be said: "The holy spirit has appointed you." (Acts 20:28) Then the newly appointed elder or elders, as notified by use of the facilities of the Watch Tower Society, may share in shepherding the congregation along with those who were already doing so, and any who have been appointed as ministerial servants may care for the duties now entrusted to them.

As long as elders measure up to the Bible's requirements for those so appointed, they may continue to serve as elders in the congregation in which their appointment is made. However, if they were to move to another congregation, they would not automatically be viewed as elders there. They would have to establish their spiritual qualifications by their Christian activity there, and then the local elders would be in position to recommend such ones for appointment in that congregation. This is also true of ministerial servants.

If an elder or ministerial servant were ever to engage in unchristian conduct of such a nature that he was disfellowshiped or was, because of wrongdoing, restricted in the assignments and duties that he could perform, the local body of elders would remove him as an elder or ministerial servant. Notification of this action would always be sent to the branch office of the Watch Tower Society. However, if he was simply unable to do some of the work, because of sickness or old age, this would not affect his appointment as an elder or ministerial servant.

The governing body may appoint men who qualify as elders to serve as overseers in any locality at any time. The governing body is not bound by the recommendations of any local group. Such recommendations serve merely as a guide, and may even be rejected for reasons well known to the governing body.—1 Tim. 1:3; Titus 1:5.

THE BODY OF ELDERS

What is the relationship of the elders to one another within a congregation? Christ is the one whom Jehovah has appointed to be Head of the congregation, so none of the elders occupies this position. None holds authority over the others. When writing to Timothy, Paul makes reference to a "body of elders" as having taken certain action. (1 Tim. 4:14, *margin*) All the elders in a congregation, as subordinates of Christ, serve together as a body of overseers or shepherds, cooperating for the advancement of the Kingdom interests and for the good of the entire congregation. —Eph. 4:15, 16; 1 Cor. 4:1, 2.

The equality of position and authority of the elders, however, does not mean that all are equal in qualities or abilities. These are bound to vary, some showing greater strengths in one direction, others in another. Some, because of age, years of Christian service, depth of Scriptural knowledge, especially good judgment in certain fields, or other qualities, may be particularly esteemed by the congregation as well as by their fellow elders. Thus, Paul said that there were "outstanding men" among the elders at Jerusalem, and he names James, Peter (Cephas) and John as ones who "seemed to be pillars." (Gal. 2:2, 9) The expression "seemed to be" indicates that they were not appointed to some superior position but were esteemed as such.

Similarly, within any body of elders there may be some whose voices will receive added attention because of the esteem in which they are held. Yet this does not make them superior or infallible. Even Peter, one of those who "seemed to be pillars," was later corrected by Paul (a man with fewer years as a disciple) for having a wrong viewpoint leading to wrong conduct.—Gal. 2:11-14.

When meetings of any kind are held, these should be conducted in an orderly manner. (1 Cor. 14:33, 40) Having someone to preside aids greatly in this. According to the Bible record, Peter evidently presided as chairman at early meetings in Jerusalem. (Acts

1:15-22; 2:1-14; 5:1-3) But this did not make him superior to the other brothers. When people in Samaria accepted the good news, the record says that the apostles, evidently acting as a body, "dispatched Peter and John to them." Thus Peter himself was subject to the direction of the body as a whole. (Acts 8:14) On the occasion of the meeting in Jerusalem to determine the circumcision issue, James, rather than Peter, offered the recommendation that was adopted by the group assembled. (Acts 15:13-21) And later James is again given prominent mention in connection with a meeting of the elders in Jerusalem. (Acts 21:18) So, evidently there was some rotation of the chairmanship. No details are given as to just how long a chairman presided, but it seems good in the congregations today to have a new chairman once a year, in all congregations where there is more than one elder.

A fine model for a meeting of the body of elders is provided in Acts chapter fifteen, where the governing body, composed of apostles and older men, is reported as having met. It is notable that at the conclusion of the conference, the governing body wrote to the congregations: "The *holy spirit* and we ourselves have favored adding no further burden to you, except these necessary things." (Acts 15:28) So, while the governing body discussed the matter, they recognized that it was God's holy spirit that guided them to their decision. Testimony was heard on that occasion from Peter, Paul and Barnabas as to the things accomplished through them by God's holy spirit. James called to mind the spirit-inspired prophecy at Amos 9:11, 12, and the holy spirit enabled this body of men to understand clearly the meaning of Amos' words recorded centuries beforehand. The result was that, with the delivering of the decision by letter to other congregations, they "continued to be made firm in the faith and to increase in number from day to day." (Acts 16:4, 5) Bodies of elders today can also count on the aid of God's holy spirit in answer to their prayers.—Luke 11:13.

It is suggested that the body of elders in each congregation meet to discuss their work about every three months. This might be done at a convenient time around the beginning of September, December,

March and June. Of course, they may convene at any time in between when circumstances make it advisable. But the arrangement for regular meetings at least every three months can aid them measurably in their efforts to work together as a body.

When the body of elders meet together to consider matters involving the flock of God, they should pray for Jehovah's direction through his Son, the Head of the congregation. (Acts 1:24, 25; 20:17, 36) Being united in their desire to advance, not their personal interests, but Kingdom interests, and having a humble viewpoint of themselves, they will be aided to speak freely among themselves and to arrive at wise decisions. —Rom. 12:3-5; 1 Cor. 1:10; Phil. 2:2-8.

Not only the chairman, but all the elders are overseers and shepherds of the "flock." All should actively promote the welfare of the congregation. So all are encouraged to take the initiative to present for consideration by the body of elders any matters that they realize need attention. And when other elders bring up points for discussion, it is to be expected that all will take an active interest.

It is the responsibility of the chairman, of course, to preside at these meetings of the elders. In doing so, he should keep in mind the apostolic injunction: "He that presides, let him do it in real earnest." (Rom. 12:8) He may prepare a program or agenda, scheduling the matters to be discussed and seeing that adequate time is allotted for each. At the meeting he may call on the various elders who brought up certain matters to make the initial presentation of them, if that seems to be most advantageous. Then others can be invited to express themselves. On any matter he can do much to keep the discussion moving forward by helping to keep the main points or issues to the fore, calling for discussion of them, one by one. He, along with all the other elders, can also do much to keep the discussion Scriptural, bringing to bear upon the subject any appropriate Bible texts.

At the periodic meetings of the elders, a principal matter to be given attention is the shepherding of the "flock." (1 Pet. 5:1-4) The elders can decide among themselves who is in position to give attention to the various shepherding needs of the congregation.

Public talks ought to be planned for the congregation. Which topics are most needed by the congregation? Are there any special subjects that should be developed in order to give attention to local needs? The elders will no doubt want to determine which talks they personally will be able to deliver during the coming months and what arrangements can be made for speakers on the remaining weeks. Which ones of the instruction talks will the elders handle in the Theocratic Ministry School? It may be beneficial to discuss this, so that these assignments can be balanced with other obligations. If there are matters that need special attention on the service meetings, the meeting of the body of elders provides an opportunity to work out the arrangements. Suggestions that any of the brothers have to improve the quality of the meetings, particularly the teaching that is done, could also beneficially be entertained at this meeting.

There is much to be done in preparing and presenting the congregation meetings each week, and in many localities the elders may well need the help of other brothers. At the periodic meetings of the elders they can consider who might appropriately be invited to handle some parts on the service meetings, who might help out with instruction talks, who might read paragraphs at the *Watchtower* study, and who could care for the responsibility that goes with being chairman at public meetings. They may decide to invite some ministerial servants to give public talks in their home congregations. Perhaps a brother who was an elder or a ministerial servant in another congregation has recently moved into the area and the local elders believe that the congregation would greatly benefit from the services of that one. If so, they may decide to write to the elders of the former congregation for information as to his conduct and the spirit that he displayed there. If a favorable reply is received, they may write the branch of the Watch Tower Society recommending him for appointment as an elder or as a ministerial servant in the congregation where he now resides.

It is requested that, during December each year, the elders review the situation of the pioneers (if any) in the congregation and send reports to the branch office where this may be beneficial. A form is provided for such use, indicating the information that is desired.

When they meet early in September, there are other matters that require special attention. If there are any ministerial servants who now meet the Scriptural qualifications for elders, it is requested that such recommendations for appointment be made at this time. Any brothers qualifying to become ministerial servants may be recommended to the governing body at the same time. Also, if any elders or ministerial servants should be removed from the list, whether due to death or moving away or because the body of elders has determined that they are no longer measuring up to the Scriptural requirements, notification of this should be sent to the branch office, if it has not already been done previously.

Since there is rotation of the chairmanship of the body of elders in each congregation where there is more than one elder, it becomes the due time at this meeting for the elders to notify the one who is to be their new chairman for the coming twelve months. The new chairman will then preside at all future meetings of the elders. This meeting in September is the due time for the body of elders to notify who of their number will care for the other positions of oversight in the congregation during the year to come. In addition to notifying the presiding overseer, notification should be given to the respective ones who are to be the field overseer, the Bible study overseer, the *Watchtower* study conductor, the Theocratic Ministry School overseer, and book study conductors for each of the book study groups. According to rotation the former overseer of the Theocratic Ministry School moves to the position of the *Watchtower* study conductor, the *Watchtower* study conductor to the position of the Bible study overseer, the Bible study overseer moves to the position of field overseer, and the field overseer moves to the position of the presiding overseer. The former presiding overseer then moves to any open position, such as congregation book study conductor.

Some individual elders in some congregations may not be able for personal reasons to conform to this pattern of rotation. In such cases the body of elders will decide what to do, still recognizing the rotation system.

In many congregations, due to a shortage of qualified brothers, elders who are able to do so may be requested to handle more than one assignment of overseership. In some cases the body of elders may request ministerial servants to help out by caring as substitutes for certain duties of overseers or as substitute study conductors.

If it seems beneficial to shift book study conductors from one study group to another for the next year, this would be an appropriate time to consider the matter. Such rotation has certain benefits, but local circumstances may not make it advantageous. The body of elders should handle the arrangements with consideration for the individuals involved.

Annually, in September, is a good time for the body of elders to review the various assignments entrusted to the ministerial servants. There is need for capable persons to care for the accounts, magazines, other literature supplies, assigning of territory, perhaps the operating of sound equipment, cleaning and upkeep of the Kingdom Hall, and service as an attendant at Kingdom Hall meetings. Some records that come under the supervision of the elders, as well as the making out of schedules, may also require considerable work. Decisions need to be made as to who will care for such necessary work during the year, allowing the elders to give as full attention as possible to shepherding and to "the ministry of the word."—Acts 6:1-6.

In some congregations there may be enough ministerial servants so that a different one can be assigned to each of these duties. Elsewhere, someone may care for several assignments. In some instances it would be beneficial to have more than one person assigned to share in certain work. (If there are not enough ministerial servants to care for these responsibilities, the body of elders may, in some cases, request younger brothers or certain sisters who show godly humility and devotion to Jehovah to assist in doing some of this necessary work, though they would not be appointed as ministerial servants.) The elders may decide that from year to year it would be beneficial to shift some ministerial servants from one assignment to another; in some cases they may ask a brother to continue to handle the same assignment. It is up to the body of elders to work out these matters in whatever manner seems to be best for the congregation.

The shifting of duties from one elder to the other should take place during the month of September regardless of whether an appointee to service has had up till then a full year in that position or not. Where a vacancy occurs in an overseer's position sometime during the year, a substitute from any of the elders can be selected by the body of elders to fill out the expiring term.

When deciding who will care for various responsibilities during the coming year, whether as elders or as ministerial servants, the elders may have in mind some new ones who are then being recommended to the governing body through the branch office for appointment. Until a reply is received on newly qualified ones, however, it would be well to hold off on the making of definite assignments of these new ones. The already existing arrangements can continue in force until the congregation is notified of new appointments.

In harmony with the Scriptures, the local body of elders has a great responsibility in connection with the shepherding of the flock of God entrusted to their care. The governing body, in accord with the requirements in the Scriptures, makes the actual appointment of elders and ministerial servants. But it is then up to the body of elders to determine, with recognition of the rotation system, who will be the presiding overseer in their congregation, and who will care for the various other positions of oversight. They also make the assignments of specific duties to the ministerial servants. These are not submitted to the governing body for appointment. This agrees with the arrangement in the early Christian congregation, because there is no evidence that the governing body assigned all the specific duties to be performed by each elder and ministerial servant in all the congregations. Those matters were evidently worked out locally.

It is requested that, as soon as possible after the body of elders has made its selection, they notify the branch office of the full name, complete mailing address and phone number (if they have such) of those brothers who will be the presiding overseer, the field overseer and the Bible study overseer for the year to come. This will assist the office to keep in touch with the congregation and direct its correspondence to the presiding overseer.

It is also recommended that, in the interest of good order, brief notes be made on each of the meetings of the body of elders, noting particularly the decisions made. The chairman may request someone from among the elders to do this, and then the notes, bearing the date of the meeting, should be retained in the congregation files.

While the elders do work together as a body, it is beneficial for each of them to be assigned to areas of special responsibility. In any body the various members fulfill differing functions, otherwise there would be no body. The apostle Paul shows that this is true of the Christian congregation, which is the body of Christ. (1 Cor. 12:12, 14, 19; Rom. 12:4-8) The same principle applies to the body of elders. Briefly, here are the responsibilities of the various overseers.

PRESIDING OVERSEER

The presiding overseer is to help coordinate the activity of all the elders so that they accomplish the most good as they work together to carry out their joint responsibility in shepherding the "flock." The responsibilities of the presiding overseer include a deep concern for the welfare of all who are associated with the congregation.

As an overseer, he should take the initiative to see that things get done. He should regularly discuss matters with the other overseers and with the ministerial servants, offering suggestions and listening to their recommendations. When problems arise, he is to take the initiative in seeing that they are given needed attention.

There are many matters that come up from week to week on which decisions must be made. It is to be expected that the presiding overseer will make appropriate decisions in order to keep the affairs of the congregation moving ahead.

However, in regard to those matters that properly are handled by the entire body of elders, the presiding overseer should submit these for attention to the body of elders. He should be well aware of the various matters that require attention in the congregation and see that they are cared for.

A principal responsibility of the presiding overseer is to be a shepherd of the "flock." He does not do this to the exclusion of participation in the field ministry, but he does give priority to caring for those who have already given indication of their desire to be associated with the congregation of Jehovah's people. He endeavors to encourage those who are showing zeal in their ministry. He also bears in mind what the apostle Paul said to the older men of the early Ephesus congregation: "I have exhibited to you in all things that by thus laboring you must assist those who are weak," and he is glad to offer such assistance. (Acts 20:35) If any feel burdened down and in need of counsel, he will endeavor to strengthen and refresh them, in imitation of Christ Jesus, our "chief shepherd."—Matt. 11:28-30.

To keep in close touch with all who are associated with the congregation, in some places the presiding overseer may find it advantageous to visit the various book study groups once or twice during the year, spending a week or a number of weeks with each one. This affords opportunity to associate in smaller groups and to share with different ones in the field ministry. If he is visiting a group that has an elder as the book study conductor, the regular conductor will care for the meeting. Where a ministerial servant usually conducts the study, the presiding overseer may want to observe for a time or two, with a view to helping him to improve his ability as a teacher. But after that the presiding overseer, as an elder, could beneficially conduct the study himself during the remainder of the visit.

Along with the other elders, the presiding overseer should regularly share in giving public talks in his home congregation, as well as giving instruction talks and participating in the service meeting programs. There is much that he can do in this way to help the entire congregation to understand the Scriptures clearly and to see how to apply them to their own lives.

His duties include making arrangements for an upbuilding service meeting for the congregation every week. He may personally take oversight of these meetings each week (making assignments and perhaps caring for the concluding portion of the program or some other suitable part), or he may share that responsibility with other capable brothers. In any event, it is his duty to be sure that the service meetings are prepared and presented for the congregation.

The program of public meetings also requires considerable attention on his part. Subjects and local speakers will have been decided on by the body of elders, but arrangements may have to be made for speakers to come from other congregations, and there ought to be some provision to extend suitable hospitality to guest speakers. (3 John 5-8) Additionally, competent chairmen should be assigned for these meetings. The presiding overseer may either care for these things personally or request the cooperation of other brothers in doing so.

The branch office regularly communicates with the congregation through the presiding overseer. Letters are sent to him either for reading to the entire congregation or for the attention of certain ones of the overseers. Orders sent to the branch office for literature and handbills, as well as remittance forms and other congregation correspondence, are signed by him. He also makes provision for certain items, such as appointment letters from the governing body and reports left by circuit overseers, to be retained in a permanent file.

Where there is more than one elder in the congregation, the presiding overseer cares for that position of oversight for just one year, unless there are only two elders and the disability of old age or some other circumstance makes it impossible for the other brother to serve. However, wherever possible, there should be a new presiding overseer each year.

At the end of his year as chairman of the body of elders, about September 1, it is requested that he write a report to the branch office, using the form provided. This will give his observations on what the spiritual condition of the congregation is, what has been accomplished during the past year, and what appears to be in need of attention during the months to come. This is not a report from the entire body of elders but is the presiding overseer's report; however, it will be read to the elders at their meeting early in September before it is mailed to the branch office, and a copy will be retained in the congregation files.

As all of Jehovah's Christian witnesses do, the presiding overseer endeavors to share regularly in the field ministry. He is very much interested in the work of Kingdom-preaching and disciple-making. He also has personal obligations that require attention. He may be secularly employed, providing for himself and his family, and that often requires considerable time. If he has a family, he needs to spend time to care for their physical, emotional and spiritual needs. (1 Tim. 5:8) He also needs opportunities for personal study. So he is not able to spend all his time in caring for congregation matters. Yet he is kind enough to arrange his affairs to extend assistance, as he is able, to all the rest of the congregation.

FIELD OVERSEER

As is true of the presiding overseer, so, too, the field overseer is an elder of the congregation, entrusted by God with responsibility to shepherd the "flock." As a teacher, he shares along with the other elders the privilege of giving public talks regularly in the congregation, also taking his turn in giving instruction talks and caring for appropriate parts on the service meeting. Additionally, he may be requested by the body of elders to conduct one of the congregation book studies each week if he has the time to do so.

The field ministry, particularly the activity of Kingdom-preaching, is a special responsibility that comes under the supervision of the field overseer. (Matt. 24:14) Much is included in this.

A certain section of territory is assigned to each congregation, and the people who live there should be visited on a regular basis with the good news. All the territory—cities, towns and rural areas—ought to be given regular attention, and the work of the field overseer includes arranging for this. In most congregations arrangements will be made for a ministerial servant to do the actual assigning of territory to those who request it and to keep the records concerning it up-to-date; but the field overseer is to check on the coverage from time to time and make needed arrangements so that all parts of the congregation's territory are given regular attention.

In caring for the oversight of Kingdom-preaching, he will help to coordinate the work so that good use is made of all the various instruments provided by the "faithful and discreet slave" class for spreading the good news. This includes making sure that suitable arrangements are made for group witnessing, and that adequate supplies of magazines and other literature are available for the congregation to use.

When notification comes from the branch office that there are to be special issues of the magazines for distribution, it is his responsibility to see that the publishers are alerted to what is being planned and are encouraged to request additional supplies that they may need. Similarly, when arrangements are made for special distribution of certain issues of the magazines or other publications to particular officials or other groups of people, the field overseer is the one who will organize the activity and see that it is carried through to a successful conclusion.

Ministerial servants will no doubt care for distribution of the magazines and other literature supplies to the publishers, but the field overseer is interested in seeing that good use is made of these instruments in the field ministry.

Of great interest to him, too, is the viewpoint with which the brothers and sisters carry on their field ministry. Both from the platform and in personal contact with them he can do much to help them to view their service as an expression of their earnest love for Jehovah and their concern for their fellowman. He should exhort them to heed the apostle's admonition, which is all the more urgent in these "last days," namely, to be "buying out the opportune time for yourselves, because the days are wicked." (Eph. 5:16) It is important to spend hours in preaching to other people, and the distribution of literature is a tremendous asset in accomplishing the preaching of the good news, but, of course, only when we are motivated by love is our service truly pleasing to God.—1 Cor. 13:1-3.

In coordinating the field ministry of the congregation, the field overseer should keep in mind that not everyone's circumstances are the same and not everyone has the same abilities. Some may be able to share in the field ministry on weekends; others, on weekdays. Certain ones may be able to spend many hours in proclaiming the good news, whereas others have obligations that limit to a considerable extent what they are able to do in this aspect of their service to God. He will help the congregation to appreciate the urgent importance of the field ministry and the value of each feature of this work, and he will gladly assist anyone to improve his ability in some aspect of the field ministry. But, instead of expecting everyone to be able to accomplish the same things, he recognizes that the entire congregation, made up of persons with a variety of gifts and abilities, works together as a united group to accomplish God's will in its assigned territory.—1 Cor. 12:14-19, 29, 30.

There are some records that come under the supervision of the field overseer. At the end of each month he collects the report cards from the pioneers (if any), tabulates the congregation's report of field ministry for the month and gives it to the presiding overseer (with the pioneer report cards) so that he can sign them and mail them to the branch office no later than the sixth of the following month. If any persons were baptized under the supervision of the congregation, instead of at an assembly, the number immersed is noted at the bottom of that congregation report. A copy of the total report of the congregation publishers is kept on a Publisher's Record card that is appropriately marked as being for the entire congregation. Then he enters on the other Publisher's Record cards each one's field service report, including the reports of regular and temporary pioneers.

If a new publisher reports field service for the first time, this makes us rejoice. But, before the report is counted, it is wise to make sure that the individual qualifies to be a publisher and that he really appreciates what it means to be publicly identified as an associate of Jehovah's Christian witnesses. So the field overseer discusses this matter with the brother or sister who is studying with the individual. He also has a personal talk with the individual, to get better acquainted with him and to commend him warmly for the progress that he is making. Then, after the field overseer discusses the matter with the presiding overseer, a record card may be made out for this new publisher and included in the congregation file, if the person qualifies.

In the event that some emergency arises calling for the attention of the body of elders at a time when the presiding overseer is away, the field overseer will act as chairman on that occasion. According to rotation, the brother who is field overseer will become the presiding overseer during the following year, starting in September.

BIBLE STUDY OVERSEER

The member of the body of elders who is assigned to be Bible study overseer has the same responsibilities as a shepherd and teacher as do the other elders in the congregation. But, in his case, the work of disciple-making, which includes making return visits and conducting home Bible studies, is a special field of activity that comes under his oversight.—Matt. 28:19, 20.

A fine place to begin in promoting home Bible study is within the households of those who are already associated with the congregation. Such study on a regular basis is a major factor in one's spiritual growth. Furthermore, it is the responsibility of fathers to 'bring up their children in the discipline and mental-regulating of Jehovah,' and a regular family Bible study helps to achieve this. (Eph. 6:4) Children do not automatically become disciples just because their parents are. They will not be followers of Christ Jesus unless they are taught the things that he commanded. Even where the household is religiously divided, it is often possible for the believer, whether the father or the mother, to study with the children. The Bible study overseer, in his contacts with members of the congregation, can do much to encourage such family study of the Bible.

He also has the responsibility to help to build up the congregation's activity in making return calls on other persons who show interest when they hear about God's kingdom. Such return visits afford opportunity to give a further witness concerning the purpose of God, and at times they open the way for a regular home Bible study. The Bible study overseer can do much to stimulate this activity by instruction on the service meeting, by personal encouragement, by arranging for those who would like help to work with others who are experienced, and by his own good example. Not everyone has equal ability as a teacher, but all in the congregation can help to locate those who desire to be taught, and the Bible study overseer can coordinate the efforts of the congregation to care for them.

He should be very much interested in all the persons who are benefiting from the congregation's teaching program through home Bible studies. Each month he will receive the Bible Study Reports that are turned in by those who are conducting studies. These do not have to be kept permanently, but they let him know exactly what is being done in this activity each month. It is good for him to keep in close touch with those who are conducting studies, to know what progress is being made and to offer suggestions when problems arise.

At congregation meetings the Bible study overseer can be a great encouragement to newcomers by putting forth a special effort to welcome them, to engage them in conversation and to answer questions that they may have. If some of these are not yet having a Bible study in their home, he can arrange that service for them. It would be a fine thing if he would get to know the name of each newly interested person who attends the meetings and show a personal interest in the progress that each one is making in his study of God's Word. This can do much to contribute to their spiritual development.

A record of the attendance is kept in connection with all the meetings of the congregation, and this is turned over to the Bible study overseer. At Kingdom Hall meetings an attendant may be requested to keep the record; at congregation book studies, it is the book study conductor who does so. Then at the end of each month a report of the attendance for each of these meetings is turned in on a Bible Study Report slip. This information is used from time to time by the elders, so the Bible study overseer is requested to make note of it, doing so in any manner that will assure a reliable record.

CONGREGATION COMMITTEE

The presiding overseer, the field overseer and the Bible study overseer constitute a service committee for handling certain matters on behalf of the congregation. For example, they check all applications for regular pioneer service, and if the applicant meets the requirements they recommend him to the branch office for appointment. They also make appointments of temporary pioneers. And when territory adjustments need to be worked out with another congregation, these brothers can usually handle the matter. Of course, if there is some question on which they believe that it would be beneficial to consult with the rest of the elders, they may do that.

In congregations where the presiding overseer, the field overseer and the Bible study overseer are all appointed elders, and none are serving in a substitute capacity, they also constitute a judicial committee. If there are not three elders in the congregation, then they may request that an elder from a nearby congregation sit with them to hear any cases requiring their attention. Their responsibility is twofold: To keep the congregation clean and in good standing before Jehovah; also, to help those who get spiritually sick, to safeguard them from straying away from the flock of God. Whenever possible, they seek to assist persons who sincerely want to serve Jehovah acceptably, but they are also well aware of the obligation not to ignore Jehovah's righteous judicial decisions.—1 Cor. 5:12–6:6; Gal. 6:1; Ps. 119:106; Jas. 5:13-16.

"WATCHTOWER" STUDY CONDUCTOR

One of the elders presides as overseer, for a year at a time, at the weekly *Watchtower* study. His particular interest is in aiding the entire congregation to benefit to the full from the spiritual food that the appointed Head of the congregation, the Lord Jesus Christ, is providing through his "faithful steward" class.—Luke 12:42.

The *Watchtower* study conductor can be of the greatest aid to the congregation if he handles the study, not merely to achieve a routine coverage of the material, but with teaching in view. To do this, he needs to set aside time to make a special study of each lesson.

This may involve going over the material several times to get it clearly in mind. Having done this, he will be able to handle the meeting in such a way that the main points are emphasized and clearly understood and the congregation is aided to discern the application in their lives of the things being learned.—Prov. 4:7.

His responsibility as a shepherd and teacher, of course, does not end with conducting the *Watchtower* study each week. He has the same general shepherding responsibilities as do the presiding overseer and the other elders in the congregation. So his duties include aiding members of the congregation on a personal basis. This may involve offering further explanation of certain points from the study material, also providing help and encouragement to those who need assistance to participate in the meeting, so that they will thus benefit more fully from this provision. It likewise includes giving warm commendation to those who are doing well, and showing active interest in any of the "sheep" that appear to be in need of attention from a shepherd who is concerned for their welfare.

His activity as a teacher also includes the giving of public talks, instruction talks and counsel on the service meeting from time to time. However, since one of his principal responsibilities is to preside at the *Watchtower* study, he may want to limit to some extent the number of public talks that he agrees to give outside his home congregation during the year so that he can give his assignment the attention that it deserves. On those occasions when it is necessary for him to be away, however, he should make sure that arrangements are made for another one of the elders to care for the meeting.

THEOCRATIC MINISTRY SCHOOL OVERSEER

As his responsibility for a year, one of the elders is delegated to the oversight of the congregation's Theocratic Ministry School. In this capacity he has opportunity to do much to enrich the congregation's knowledge and appreciation of the Scriptures, also to help them to improve their abilities individually as preachers and teachers.

The outline of material covered in the school is provided each year through the branch office, and the Theocratic Ministry School overseer follows this in making assignments to those who have enrolled in the school. Usually these assignments are made at least three weeks in advance so that the speakers will have ample time to prepare.

Counsel given to student speakers should be kind and encouraging. It is also helpful to everyone if explanation is included as to *how* certain things can be done and *why* they are effective. The remarks of the school overseer, however, will be most beneficial if they are not limited exclusively to analysis of speech qualities. He should prepare for each week's school session with the objective of helping the congregation to get full value from the fine *material* that is to be covered. Then, if principal points that are of particular interest are not covered by a speaker, or are inaccurately expressed, he will be able to draw attention to them, to the extent that time permits. He is not to try to review the contents of the talks given, but his appreciative comments on an important thought, how it was presented and the value of the information, can help to impress it on the minds of everyone. In this way, while individuals are being aided to improve as speakers and teachers, the attention of those in attendance is kept focused primarily on the Word of God.

This overseer can also help the congregation in his contacts with them as individuals. Some of the students may need help in understanding the material assigned to them and in finding a way to make practical application of it. His duties are not limited to the school, however. As a shepherd, he is desirous of aiding all in the congregation in any way that he can.

If the congregation has a large enrollment in its Theocratic Ministry School, it may be divided into two or more sections for the student talks. In this way each one can have opportunity to give a talk at least every three months. Where possible, elders will offer counsel to the students in the additional groups. These additional counselors will be selected by the Theocratic Ministry School overseer.

In most Kingdom Halls a library is provided for the use of the congregation. Usually it contains all the available publications of the Watch Tower Society, perhaps a variety of Bible translations, an exhaustive concordance and some other helpful reference works. It is cared for under the supervision of the school overseer.

CONGREGATION BOOK STUDY CONDUCTOR

Whenever possible, the brothers who conduct the congregation book studies should also be elders, because this assignment involves teaching. If there is not an elder available for each of the study groups, it may be that one of the elders can care for more than one group, doing so at different times during the week. But that depends to a considerable extent on his circumstances. If more book study conductors are needed, the local body of elders may request certain ministerial servants who give evidence of teaching ability to serve as substitute conductors, until such time as an elder is available. In each case it is the body of elders that assigns the brother to the book study group where he will preside.

The primary responsibility of each congregation book study conductor is teaching. To do a really fine job of conducting the study each week, the book study conductor usually has to spend more time in preparation than other brothers do. He needs to know, not only the answers to the study questions, but also the reasons for those answers and the value of the information. It should be his aim to help those who attend the study to understand, to be able to explain and to apply in their lives the truths studied. This requires conscientious effort on the part of the study conductor. As the apostle Paul wrote: "He that teaches, let him be at his teaching."—Rom. 12:7.

The book study conductor also has the privilege of aiding the publishers in his group in their Kingdom-preaching and discipling work. He can do much to help those in his group to show enthusiastic appreciation for the privilege of participating in this activity. He should endeavor to make arrangements for group witnessing at times that are convenient to those in the group, and he should be sure that there is territory on hand for them to work. When it is possible for him to be with them, he will take the lead at the meeting for field service and in organizing the work to be done in the territory. For those times when he is not able to be there, he will endeavor to arrange for a ministerial servant to care for the group, or, if none is available, then another publisher who is willing to accept that responsibility.

Since each book study conductor is assigned to care for a relatively small group, he can usually become well acquainted with all of those who attend the study. As a shepherd, he ought to show a warm interest in each one of them, giving personal help and encouragement to them in their field ministry, as respects the congregation meetings and in other aspects of Christian living. If any are ill or depressed, he will probably know that and can pay them a visit to build them up. If some can be aided to reach out for additional privileges of service, he should be alert to assist them. Much of the attention of the book study conductor will be directed toward helping those in his own group, but, if he is an elder, his shepherding responsibilities are not limited to them. To the extent possible, he should endeavor to show concern for the entire congregation, reaching out to aid any of the "sheep" according to their needs.

CITY OVERSEER

Where there is more than one congregation in a city, the branch office deals with each congregation separately, sending supplies directly to it and receiving its monthly service report. However, one of the elders is also appointed by the Watch Tower Society's branch office as city overseer. This is not an appointment that changes each year. He does not exercise any jurisdiction in any congregation other than the one where he serves as an elder. However, the branch office may wish to communicate with him at times in connection with arrangements for assemblies and other matters. He may also be called on by the elders of other congregations for counsel if some special need arises.

CIRCUIT OVERSEER

To assist all the congregations, it has proved beneficial for circuit overseers to spend some time with them on a regular basis. The circuit overseers are traveling elders who are appointed by the Watch Tower Society to their circuit position. During their visit they meet with the body of elders and cooperate with them in caring for the portion of the "flock" in their care. They give a variety of discourses to the congregation. And there are daily arrangements for group witnessing with them.

The congregations visited by a circuit overseer are termed a circuit. The circuit overseer plans his route so that he will be able to visit each congregation about once every six months, serving them for about five and a half days on each occasion. In the case of pioneers, special pioneers and missionaries in isolated territory, he also stays for a full week with them, aiding and encouraging them by holding meetings, working in the field service with them and studying together.

When the congregation is notified of a visit by the circuit overseer, about two months in advance, the presiding overseer makes the needed preparations for the visit. Since his visit will be a time of increased activity in the field ministry, additional magazines may be ordered, including what the circuit overseer has requested for himself. Handbills will no doubt be ordered for the public talk that he is to give. These things ought to be done early. Then sleeping accommodations and meals need to be arranged for the visiting overseer and his wife, if he is married.

As his visit draws near, the presiding overseer arranges times for special meetings to be held with the congregation, with the pioneers and with the body of elders. Locations from which field service will be carried out need to be selected, along with territory in which to work. The presiding overseer plans for a full schedule of field service during the week with the publishers. Then, just before his visit, congregation records are gathered together at the Kingdom Hall.

On his arrival at a congregation, the circuit overseer spends Tuesday afternoon consulting the congregation records. He may read over the end-of-the-year report sent to the branch office by the former presiding overseer, and acquaint himself with the congregation to some extent by examining the Publisher's Record cards. He also examines the territory file and the congregation accounts, and takes note of the care given to literature supplies in the congregation. Sometime that day he sees the presiding overseer, to receive from him details concerning the program of activity for the week.

Later in the week, at a convenient time, the entire body of elders will meet with the circuit overseer. He is present, not to pass judgment on what the congregation has been doing nor to make changes, but to work along with the body of elders, for he, too, is an elder. (1 Pet. 5:1) As is customary at meetings of the elders, the local presiding overseer will be chairman. The presiding overseer will no doubt have listed in advance the matters on which they would appreciate helpful observations or counsel from the circuit overseer. The circuit overseer, too, may have noted matters that he believes it would be beneficial to discuss. These various topics or questions may be submitted to the chairman, who will call for discussion of them in a reasonable order. He may introduce certain matters himself, or he may ask another elder who is personally acquainted with the situation to do so. The circuit overseer will be invited to offer any counsel that he believes will be helpful. It is not expected that he will know the answer to every question or that he will have a background of experience with every type of situation that may arise, but he is glad to share the information that he does have. Others of the elders should feel free to ask questions and to offer observations.

In some cases what is needed is counsel on spiritual matters, and this, of course, should come from God's Word. In other cases the brothers may simply be seeking some advice that is based on practical experience, whether that of the circuit overseer or of the brothers in the congregations that he has served. The length of this meeting is determined to a considerable extent by what needs to be discussed.

If there are any matters on which individuals associated with the congregation would like to have counsel from the circuit overseer, they too should feel free to approach him during his visit. He is an "older man," a shepherd of God's "flock," and he comes to the congregation to be of help in any way that he can.

During the week of his visit all the congregation meetings will be held at their normal times, and will be conducted by those regularly assigned to do so. The circuit overseer will attend these meetings and benefit from them along with the rest of the congregation.

On a number of occasions, however, he will address the ones assembled. For example, at the congregation book study that he attends, the one presiding may conclude the study ten minutes early that evening and invite the visiting circuit overseer to offer any words of encouragement that he may have for the group. (Compare Acts 13:15.) Similarly, on the service meeting the final half hour will be assigned to him to give a discourse.

Toward the end of the week he will conduct a special program lasting about an hour and fifteen minutes. Part of this program is a stimulating discussion of new things learned, covering information in *Watchtower* issues of the previous six months (also Scriptural articles in *Awake!*) and any of the bound books of the Watch Tower Society released during the past twelve months, while another part of the program is a Scriptural talk. At the regular time set aside for it, he also gives the public talk, one that has been especially designed for his use. And at the conclusion of the final meeting with the entire congregation he delivers another Scriptural discourse, about thirty minutes in length.

He is not present in the congregation to analyze the congregation's service record and pronounce it weak or strong, but to upbuild the brothers, and he has a fine opportunity to do this in his discourses. These are to be Scriptural discussions, helping those present to appreciate and strengthen their relationship to Jehovah and to Christ Jesus. He can aid the congregation to see the whole scope of the Christian ministry, the many opportunities that there are for them individually to advance the interests of pure worship. He can build up their appreciation for the grand privilege of serving Jehovah, and share with them helpful suggestions and encouraging experiences related to such service.—Acts 15:3.

For five days of his visit, Wednesday through Sunday, the circuit overseer will spend a large proportion of his time in the field ministry with the brothers and sisters. He has had much experience in the field ministry, and he is with the congregation to share the benefits of that experience with them, to assist them in any appropriate way to further the work of preaching and disciple-making. This is one of the principal reasons why he is sent to the congregation. The presiding overseer should notify the congregation in advance as to where and when the meetings for field service will be held, and encourage all who can to join in group witnessing during the week. It is beneficial for the publishers to arrange for some time to be spent in door-to-door activity and some in making return visits. If anyone would especially like to have an appointment to go from door to door with him or to have assistance with return visits or in a home Bible study, the individual can mention this to the presiding overseer, and he will gladly arrange it with the circuit overseer. Apart from those arrangements, the circuit overseer may work out his own schedule of accompanying publishers in the field ministry, depending on who is present at the meetings for group witnessing.

If the circuit overseer is married, his wife will devote as many hours as she can to the field service. She works under the direction of her husband, and in most cases he is glad to arrange for her to accompany sisters in the congregation in the field service.

Before leaving the congregation, but after his meeting with the body of elders, the circuit overseer fills out a report to the branch office on what service he rendered during his visit, making observations on the spiritual condition of the congregation, matters that were discussed with the elders, and so forth. He leaves a copy of this report with the presiding overseer of the congregation.

If he observes a seriously unhealthy spiritual condition, or finds that the plain counsel of God's Word is not being applied in the congregation, he will, of course, discuss the matter with the body of elders, and after having done this, he may take it up in one of his talks to the entire congregation. This too would be included in his report.

If serious wrongdoing develops in a congregation, and the local body of elders is remiss in shouldering its responsibility to safeguard the "flock of God" and to uphold pure worship, the Watch Tower Society through its branch representatives has the authority to send one or more elders (perhaps including a circuit overseer) into the congregation to examine the situation and make its report and recommendation to the branch. —Acts 15:22; 16:4, 5.

Twice a year two-day circuit assemblies are arranged for the benefit of the congregations. The circuit overseer is responsible for the operation of the assembly organization on these occasions. On the circuit overseer's recommendation, the Society appoints various permanent assembly personnel: an assembly overseer, an assistant assembly overseer and a news representative. They are to work closely with the circuit overseer in caring for the assembly organization, so that the circuit overseer can give his primary attention to the assembly program. Other capable men, too, may be designated by the circuit overseer to care for various departments.

At the close of each month when the circuit overseer and his wife send their field service reports to the branch office, they also submit a report on expenses incurred, provided they were not covered by the congregations. Such expenses for which the branch office reimburses the circuit overseer include transportation. The branch office will also cover food and lodging, if some congregations are not able to make provision. In addition, a small monthly allowance is sent for personal things, and the fact that they obtain literature at pioneer rates provides a little more to keep them going in the work. They have confidence that, as Jesus promised, if they seek continually the interests of Jehovah's kingdom, the material needs will be provided. —Luke 12:31.

DISTRICT OVERSEER

Another one of the traveling elders of Jehovah's Christian witnesses is the district overseer. He, too, is appointed by the Society, and is assigned by the branch office to the section where he serves. His assignment includes participation in the program at circuit assemblies, as well as service with a congregation in the area where each assembly is held.

A number of circuits comprise a district. After corresponding with the circuit overseers as to dates when assembly facilities may be available, the branch office plans the schedule of the district overseer so that he will be able to serve each of the assemblies in his district. In some circuits, due to travel distance or the size of available assembly facilities, more than one assembly is arranged, and the district overseer is scheduled to spend one week in the circuit for each assembly held. Such circuit assemblies, each two days in length, are held twice a year.

On Tuesday afternoon, at the beginning of his visit, he meets with the circuit overseer and his wife (if he is married). In connection with their ministry, the circuit overseer may have in mind certain matters that he would like to discuss, and the district overseer will no doubt have helpful information that he can share. This is also an opportunity for the district overseer to learn about any special needs that the circuit may have, so that he can take them into consideration in his remarks at the forthcoming assembly. During the remainder of that week the circuit overseer will no doubt be busy much of the time with assembly arrangements, though he will probably be able to arrange some time to work in the field ministry with the district overseer.

Since the district overseer will also be working during the week with a congregation in the assembly city (unless instructed by the branch office to work with a congregation elsewhere), he needs to get in touch with the presiding overseer of that congregation sometime on Tuesday. The congregation usually is notified well in advance by the circuit overseer so they can arrange to show hospitality to the district overseer (and his wife, if he is married) by providing accommodations and meals, if possible. Before his visit the presiding overseer will also have made plans for the week's activity, and the presiding overseer will provide necessary details to the district overseer. He is there to help the congregation in any way possible.

One of his principal duties while with the congregation is to take the lead in arrangements for group witnessing, usually from Wednesday through Friday. On those days he is ordinarily able to devote most of his time to the field ministry, participating in both door-to-door preaching and the making of return visits. Where possible, he accompanies others, sharing with them practical suggestions that he has picked up over the years. To a considerable extent, he arranges his own schedule to accompany publishers in the field service, depending on who is at the meetings for group witnessing.

Participation in the field ministry thus has an important place in his schedule. He endeavors to devote as many field hours with the publishers as he can each month. If he is married, his wife does likewise.

On an evening arranged for by the presiding overseer, the district overseer gives a Scriptural talk of about an hour for the congregation that he is serving. If there are any matters on which the body of elders want his counsel, they may also arrange to meet with him for that purpose, possibly on the same evening that he speaks to the congregation. Of course, some evenings will probably be used in rehearsing parts for the circuit assembly.

During the two days of the circuit assembly, there is much for the district overseer to do. He is the assembly chairman, responsible to see that the program runs smoothly. He himself has a number of talks to give, including the public discourse.

At the conclusion of the assembly the district overseer sends a report to the branch office, making note of matters discussed with the circuit overseer, also with the elders gathered at the assembly, as well as his observations on the circuit assembly and the spiritual condition of the circuit itself. His accommodations, expenses and field ministry reports are cared for in the same way as those for the circuit overseer.

There is a rotation of assignments of the traveling elders every two years. This may involve a rotation of one from being a district overseer to circuit overseer and vice versa.

BRANCH OVERSEER

The branch overseer is an elder who is appointed by the Watch Tower Society and has general oversight of the congregations of Jehovah's witnesses in an entire country or group of lands.

He arranges for the sending out of literature provided by the "faithful and discreet slave," and supervises the preaching and disciple-making work in such a way that people in all the territory under the branch office are given opportunity to hear the good news. He sees that needed attention is given to all the congregations, circuit and district overseers, regular and special pioneers as well as missionaries, and he personally serves on assembly programs in various parts of the land.

The appointment of a branch overseer is for an indefinite time, until the Watch Tower Society may see fit to replace him.

ZONE OVERSEER

Arrangements are made by the Watch Tower Society for persons who are elders to visit the Society's branch offices and printing plants as well as all the missionary homes of Jehovah's witnesses throughout the world. These visiting elders are known as zone overseers.

As overseers, they do a work of visiting and inspecting. They examine the records of each branch, analyze its oversight of the congregations under its jurisdiction and what is being accomplished in preaching the good news and making disciples. They attend congregation meetings with the branch overseer and the missionaries and, where possible, accompany them in the field ministry. They are interested in the spiritual condition of those whom they serve and in what is being done by the shepherds in caring for the "flock of God."

So, there is, indeed, an interchange of encouragement throughout all the congregations of God, all being bound together in unity through love and the spirit of God. (Rom. 1:12; Eph. 4:3; Col. 3:14) Everyone in the "flock of God" is strengthened with a sense of interdependency, just as the various parts of the human body serve for the common good of the whole body. (1 Cor. 12:12-31) And as each one is drawn close to his fellow servants in loving unity, he is also brought closer to Christ Jesus the appointed Head of the Christian congregation, and to Jehovah God, whose spirit permeates the entire congregation and whose Word guides its operation in harmony with his righteous purpose.—Eph. 1:22, 23; Prov. 3:5, 6.

CHAPTER 5

MEETINGS AT WHICH TO BE TAUGHT BY JEHOVAH

THE psalmist David, a man after God's own heart, long ago wrote: "I rejoiced when they were saying to me: 'To the house of Jehovah let us go.'" (Ps. 122:1) At the "house of Jehovah" instruction was given in the law of God, psalms of praise were sung and there was opportunity to give expression of one's own appreciation for Jehovah's loving-kindness. Meetings for worship continue to have an important place in the lives of Jehovah's Christian witnesses and to be a source of real enjoyment to them.

It is true that during his earthly life Jesus did not institute among his disciples any special program of weekly meetings. He himself was born under the Law, and he kept the requirements of the Law. He attended the annual festivals prescribed by the Law, and he was regularly on hand at the local synagogue for the program of reading and teaching from the Scriptures. Additionally, he personally gave discourses to large gatherings of people, and there were occasions when he especially instructed his disciples about the preaching work that they were to do. (Matt. 4:23; 5:1, 2; Luke 10:1-16) But they were still part of God's congregation of natural Israel.

However, following the outpouring of the holy spirit on Jesus' disciples at Pentecost, 33 C.E., Christian congregations began to spring up in one locality after another. These were now the people upon whom God had put his spirit, and they regularly met together. The Bible does not describe in detail each of the meetings that they had in their congregations. But we do know that they considered in written form material that is now part of the Holy Bible. (Col. 4:16; Rev. 2:1; 3:1) We also know from the Scripture record that they were provided with instructions on how to conduct their meetings in a way befitting the people of God. Among them were teachers who worked hard on their behalf.—1 Cor. 14:26-33; 1 Tim. 5:17; Acts 13:1.

The teaching, of course, really came from Jehovah himself, because it was his inspired Word that provided the basis for what was said. It was as the prophet Isaiah had written: "All your sons will be persons taught by Jehovah, and the peace of your sons will be abundant." Jesus applied that prophecy to his own disciples.—Isa. 54:13; John 6:45.

Appropriately, the meetings of Jehovah's witnesses are opened and closed with prayer, because we look to Jehovah for his blessing and guidance and we are thankful for his provisions. (1 Chron. 29:10; 1 Cor. 14:15, 16; Matt. 18:20) This is true whether the meetings are ones attended only by regular members of the congregation or are ones to which the public has been specially invited. If two meetings are held, one after the other, then prayer is offered at the beginning and at the end of the entire program.

During congregation discussions in which the audience is invited to participate, it is a privilege to have a share. Of Jesus Christ, it was prophetically written: "I will declare your name to my brothers; in the middle of the congregation I shall praise you." (Ps. 22:22; Heb. 2:12) He set the example for us to imitate. Not only out in the world among unbelievers, but also when with our brothers, we should speak of the grand things that Jehovah has done and will yet do. The apostle Paul urged: "Let us hold fast the public declaration of our hope . . . And let us consider one another to incite to love and fine works." (Heb. 10:23, 24) It is true that we may be inclined to feel that others give better comments than we do. But our public declaration of faith is upbuilding to them, warming their hearts. It shows our genuine love because, no matter how little we personally feel that we have, we are willing to share it with others. This truly is pleasing to God.

Those having children should not hesitate to bring them to the meetings—even the little ones. As Moses commanded Israel: "Congregate the people, the men and the women and the little ones . . . in order that they may listen and in order that they may learn, as they must fear Jehovah your God and take care to carry out all the words of this law." (Deut. 31:12)

The good results of early training are indicated in the case of Timothy, a zealous associate of the apostle Paul and one who had been taught the holy writings from infancy.—2 Tim. 3:14, 15.

By attending meetings we all learn practical application of God's Word. For this same reason it is good to be enthusiastic about inviting fellow workmen, relatives, neighbors and others to attend the meetings with you. When they hear what is discussed, and see the love manifested among those in attendance, they too may be moved to declare: "God is really among you."—1 Cor. 14:25.

Consider, now, each of the meetings provided in the congregations of Jehovah's Christian witnesses, how they benefit us personally and how they equip us to share in the great work of Kingdom-preaching and disciple-making.

THE "WATCHTOWER" STUDY

The principal publication that the "faithful and discreet slave" class has used in more recent times to provide Jehovah's people with spiritual food drawn from God's Word is the *Watchtower* magazine. So each congregation arranges to meet once a week to study a portion of this material under the chairmanship of the *Watchtower* study conductor.

Usually the *Watchtower* study is held following a public meeting that was opened with song and prayer. Between the meetings the entire congregation is customarily invited to share in singing a song before the *Watchtower* study begins. The *Watchtower* study conductor, at the outset, makes some brief comments to whet the audience's appetite for what is to follow and to help them to appreciate the reason for considering the specific material at hand. If it is a continuation of an article started the previous week, he may briefly restate certain key points from that earlier study and tie them in with what is next to be considered. The printed questions provided in *The Watchtower* are propounded, then the study conductor calls on those who volunteer by raising their hands for their answers. During the discussion he may helpfully direct attention to the scriptures in the paragraph, encouraging comments that show their relation to the question being considered. If time allows, he also calls for the reading of certain scriptures that are cited but not quoted. The paragraphs are read in summary. For reading the paragraphs a different reader may be used each week and, if possible, advance selection is made of a baptized brother who reads well.

Ordinarily, the *Watchtower* study is just one hour in length, with about ten additional minutes for the opening and closing, including announcements. By having comments ready to offer as soon as the questions are asked, you can help to keep the study moving and make it possible for the congregation to hear many helpful expressions on the material during the time set aside for the study.

In most cases the entire congregation gathers together at the Kingdom Hall for their weekly *Watchtower* study. However, if some live at distant points, far from the Kingdom Hall, *Watchtower* studies are sometimes arranged for them by the body of elders, who appoint a study conductor. These studies may be either on Sunday or another day that is convenient for them. It is better to have a *Watchtower* study in their own locality than for them to miss it because of the long distance and inconvenience in traveling to the central meeting. In such cases, usually a brother living in that vicinity is assigned as the study conductor.

The meeting is held in the language of the country or district, unless the congregation was specifically organized to serve a different language group. However, if there is a group of persons in the congregation who speak another tongue, there is no objection to arranging a *Watchtower* study for the benefit of these brothers. The body of elders will select the one to conduct this meeting. They will get a clearer understanding by studying *The Watchtower* in their own language and expressing themselves in their own tongue. The extra-language meetings should be at a time different from the regular meetings for the congregation, however, and those attending these meetings should also be encouraged to attend the regular meetings of the congregation, to get acquainted with the language of the land where they dwell. In this way they will, in time, be able to have a more extensive share in the field ministry.

THE PUBLIC MEETING

The public meeting is quite different from the *Watchtower* study. Rather than being a question-and-answer discussion of printed study material, it generally takes the form of a discourse. But to stimulate keen interest and to impress key thoughts on the minds of everyone, the speaker may use pictures, maps or an outline of points on a blackboard. As part of the program, arrangements may be made for questions both to and from the audience. At times, the material may be presented by a symposium of speakers.

Those who give the public talks in the congregation will be elders, to the extent that this is possible, since these are brothers who not only set a fine example in Christian living but also are qualified teachers. (1 Tim. 3:2) Where there are only a few elders, they will find that, as was true of those with similar privileges in the first century, they "work hard in speaking and teaching" to provide this instruction for the congregation. (1 Tim. 5:17) Their willingness to give of themselves in this way is deeply appreciated by their Christian brothers. And, by way of assistance, the "faithful and discreet slave" provides the elders with printed outlines in most instances from which to develop these talks on a wide variety of subjects. To fill out their program, the local elders may also invite elders from other congregations to give talks, arranging this first through the presiding overseers of those congregations, and then confirming details in personal correspondence to the speakers.

In some areas, however, there just may not be enough elders available. If the body of elders desires to do so, they may assign ministerial servants from their own congregation to give public talks from time to time, using an outline provided by the Society, where this is necessary in order to have the public meetings on a regular basis. But no congregation will send out as a speaker to another congregation a brother who is not yet an elder.

A capable brother, generally one of the elders or the ministerial servants, is assigned in advance to be chairman at the public meeting. After he warmly welcomes those in attendance, the congregation usually joins in a song of praise to Jehovah, and then prayer is offered. Following this, the chairman informs the audience of the title of the talk to be given and introduces the speaker. His remarks are very brief. After the talk, the chairman makes whatever announcements are appropriate for those present.

If there is no meeting following the public talk, the program will be closed with song and prayer. However, if it is followed by the *Watchtower* study, as is usually the case, the final song and prayer come at the conclusion of the entire program. Between the two meetings, where there is no intermission, it is good to invite the audience to stand and sing a song. If there is an intermission, then the public meeting will be concluded with needed announcements, and, when the group reconvenes, a song may be sung before the *Watchtower* study gets under way.

In addition to putting on talks in your Kingdom Hall, arrangements may be made for holding public talks in rural sections and outlying towns in the congregation's territory. Efforts are made to give a thorough witness in this territory in conjunction with the public meetings. If there are many locations that can be obtained, such as community houses, lodge halls, schools, private homes of Jehovah's witnesses, lawns, fields and parks, the congregation will no doubt plan on using some of them. Usually they can be obtained at a very reasonable cost or even free. If you assist in setting up sound equipment for such a meeting, keep in mind that you should conform to local regulations as to operating the equipment. The loudspeakers need be loud enough to reach only the audience so that all can hear well.

These are called *public* meetings because extensive advertising is frequently done to invite the public and the talks are given with the public in mind. Not that the material is directed solely to the public, but, since newly interested ones are often present, the speaker makes it a point to explain his subject in terms that they can grasp. At the same time, the information is highly informative and upbuilding to the members of the congregation who are regular attenders. Whenever possible, arrangements are made to have these public meetings every week.

THE SERVICE MEETING

The service meeting is specifically designed to equip you to have a full share in carrying out the work of preaching the Kingdom good news and making disciples of those who respond to God's Word. (Matt. 24:14; 28:19, 20) To a large extent this work is done by speaking to other persons and providing them with Bible literature. But the application of Bible principles in our lives has a great bearing on the effectiveness of this field ministry, for thereby we demonstrate our sincerity and the good results that come from applying the Scriptures. Appropriately, the service meeting gives attention to all these facets of our service to God.

Service meetings are usually built around the information provided in *Kingdom Ministry,* which you will receive every month through the congregation. When a new issue of *Kingdom Ministry* is received, the presiding overseer carefully analyzes what it contains and either personally assigns the various meeting parts to qualified brothers or arranges for this to be done, and those assigned receive written notice.

That outline of meetings is flexible, however, and may be adjusted to emphasize aspects of our service to God that need particular attention locally. The body of elders may be aware that a certain situation needs to be handled, and they may have ideas for a program on a night for which no program is outlined by the Society.

As for the individual meeting parts, elders and ministerial servants are requested to take charge of these. They need to study the assigned material carefully, to determine what the principal points of instruction are and how to handle them so that the brothers will understand and remember them. Careful thought also ought to be given to application of the material to the situation of the local congregation. Suggestions that are presented in connection with preaching the good news should not be set out as if they were rules. There is much room for individual initiative in our activity. However, it is important to help everyone to see how the things that we do are involved in our worship, so that we all carry them out with a desire to please Jehovah.

There are many ways in which material can be effectively presented. However, in no case should the method of presentation be allowed to overshadow the material presented. The objective of demonstrations is not to have a great dramatic production with a lot of stage props. Use natural settings, such as a scene at one's secular work, a door-to-door visit, a home Bible study or a family discussion. Arrangements should be made to rehearse demonstrations, so that each participant knows where he is to be and what he is to do. Of course, this takes time, but it results in a program that is informative and spiritually upbuilding.

If each one on the program sticks to the allotted time, the meeting will conclude in about an hour, including the song and prayer. Everyone who shares in the program should cooperate to that end.

When demonstrations or discussions are included in the program, any of those attending the meetings and who are in good standing with the congregation, including children, may be invited to participate. If you are asked to assist in this way, cooperate joyfully and conscientiously, recognizing that this is part of your service to Jehovah.

THEOCRATIC MINISTRY SCHOOL

In addition to the other meetings, each congregation of Jehovah's witnesses provides a Theocratic Ministry School conducted by the Theocratic Ministry School overseer. This is a continuous school for men, women and children. As part of this course, those enrolled are encouraged to read the entire Bible according to the consecutive sections assigned from week to week. Some students give short talks to the entire group, others demonstrate how to discuss various Scriptural subjects with individuals, and a qualified counselor offers helpful suggestions for improvement.

By enrolling in the Theocratic Ministry School, which convenes once each week at the Kingdom Hall, you show that you are interested in advancement. Such instruction can aid you to be a finer public praiser of Jehovah. It can equip you to accomplish more in the time you have available for the field service, as well as to give fine comments in the congregation meetings. In the case of brothers, this instruction is of great aid to anyone striving to qualify to be a ministerial servant or an elder. Even persons newly attending the meetings may enroll, as long as they are not leading lives that are out of line with Christian principles.

Those enrolled will be assigned periodically to give student talks, and they will be notified well in advance so that they can prepare thoroughly. Though no roll call is read at the school, you will benefit greatly by being present, and particularly is it important to be on hand when you are assigned to give a talk. Plan to get to the hall before the meeting starts, so the Theocratic Ministry School overseer will know that you are present to give your talk. If an emergency situation arises, and it is impossible to be present to fulfill an assignment, be sure to notify the school overseer, doing so just as early as possible so that he can arrange for someone else to prepare the material.

After each student talk the overseer will offer helpful counsel. So, if you will be giving a talk, before the meeting be sure to give him your Speech Counsel slip, because he will want to make notations on it. If you have done well on certain qualities, he will commend you. If further work on some matter would be beneficial, he will offer suggestions to assist you. Where it appears to be advantageous, he may also make some brief comments on the Scriptural material presented, to help the congregation to get the full benefit from it and to make sure that they understand it correctly. His comments are to assist you and all the congregation to be better praisers of Jehovah.

In addition to the student talks, the school program usually includes an instruction talk. These are given preferably by the elders of the congregation; but, if they are not able to handle all of them, some of the better qualified ministerial servants may be assigned. There is usually an oral review of the previous week's instruction talk, and it will be stimulating to you, and beneficial to others too, if you prepare ahead of time and volunteer to answer at least one of these review questions. Then, too, periodically there may be a written review of the information that has been studied. Each person checks his own paper. This review is not for competitive purposes but is a means of helping you to see if you have an accurate understanding of the material that has been discussed, and it assists you to learn any key points that you may have missed.

Even those who may not, for some reason, be enrolled in the school are encouraged to attend. All who are present will benefit from the fine instruction provided.

CONGREGATION BOOK STUDY

The congregation book study is generally conducted with a smaller group than the other meetings. There are just a few families or a comparatively small number of individuals who gather at each of these studies. Instead of having the entire congregation come together at one place for the meeting, arrangements can be made for them to meet in convenient locations scattered throughout the congregation's territory. One group may meet at the Kingdom Hall; others assemble in private homes. Here is a reflection of Jehovah's loving-kindness and his tender care for his people, because in these small groups it is possible for more personal attention to be given to the spiritual growth of each individual. —Isa. 40:11.

This is a one-hour group study, using the Bible and a textbook provided by the Watch Tower Society. Basically, the meeting is conducted in the same manner as the *Watchtower* study. It is opened and closed with prayer. Questions are asked on each paragraph; comments are invited; scriptures are read; paragraphs are read in summary. However, at the congregation book study there is no set amount of material to be covered, so more time can be spent in discussing the material. To impress principal thoughts on the mind of each one, a *brief* oral review may be conducted at the end of the study.

With a small group such as this, there is more opportunity for you to comment. You will find that it is not at all difficult to participate freely at this meeting, and this gives you opportunity to get accustomed to making a declaration of your faith before others. (Heb. 13:15) It is good to learn to make your comments in your own words, instead of reading them out of the book, because this enables you to determine whether you really understand the material.

Although everyone present is encouraged to share in the reading of scriptures, just one person reads the paragraphs at any one study. If possible, arrangements are made a week in advance for a baptized brother who is a good reader to read the paragraphs.

Having these study groups scattered throughout the congregation territory makes it convenient for both you and newly interested persons in the neighborhood to attend. Endeavor to bring others with you to the meeting, so that they can get a taste of the spiritually upbuilding discussions and warm association that we here enjoy.

In addition to providing a place for group study, the location where the congregation book study is held may also be a meeting place for field service. Here the group can meet at convenient times to share in this important feature of our Christian ministry.

When your congregation book study group grows to the point where the elders may deem it wise to make adjustments, they will consider arranging for an additional study group at another location. As long as there is room to accommodate everyone, they may wait until the group includes as many as twenty regular participants in the field service before any division is made, but there are other factors to be considered too. Of course, if a new group is formed, another home will be needed where they can meet. It should be one that is neat and clean, and located where it will be convenient for a group of brothers to meet so that none will have to travel very far. Having congregation meetings in private homes was a practice of the early Christians, and it has continued to have Jehovah's blessing in our day.—Rom. 16:3, 5; Philem. 1, 2.

NEW OR SMALL CONGREGATIONS

As the preaching of the good news is accomplished and more persons identify themselves as disciples of Christ Jesus, the number of congregations also increases. Each of these congregations endeavors to arrange for all the various meetings discussed earlier.

Such new congregations may be groups of newly dedicated, baptized disciples who are gathering in places isolated from previously existing congregations. Or it may be that a congregation already in operation has grown large, or that the size of the Kingdom Hall or the distance that some travel to the meetings makes it advisable to form a new congregation.

When a new congregation is organized, those who are associated with the group make application to the branch office so that they can benefit from the services provided for all congregations of Jehovah's Christian witnesses. The matter should first be thoroughly discussed by those involved, whether a group of publishers in an isolated area, or the congregation's body of elders in the case of division of an already-existing congregation. Then, before the application is submitted, it may be advisable to discuss the matter with the circuit overseer. In some cases small groups may find it more advantageous to be associated with larger congregations that are not far distant. In any event, however, for a congregation to be recognized by the branch office, there must be a group of persons who are baptized proclaimers of the good news, persons who truly are Jehovah's Christian witnesses and who recognize the "faithful and discreet slave" class and desire to work under its direction to advance the interests of pure worship.

In naming our congregations we follow the Biblical precedent, designating each congregation by the name of the city or town in which it is located. (1 Cor. 1:2; 1 Thess. 1:1) When a congregation is divided into two or more congregations within a city, then a geographic or other designation describing its location is used as a name for each congregation.

In each congregation, large or small, the regular study procedure can be followed at the *Watchtower* study and the congregation book study. If there are not enough qualified persons to prepare all the various service meeting parts, at least they can read and discuss the material together. Similarly, adjustments can be made in the Theocratic Ministry School. If possible, it is good to arrange for the instruction talk to be given as a model talk each week. But, where necessary, the other assignments may be covered by somewhat informal reports, discussions between two sisters, questions and answers or simply reading the published information. For public meetings, local brothers can no doubt give talks from time to time. Occasionally, arrangements can probably be made for visiting speakers, and this will be a stimulus to the group. And, when no speaker is available, the group can even read together one of the extensive outlines provided by the Watch Tower Society and look up the scriptures together.

At times small congregations may be composed entirely of sisters. When such is the case, sisters who pray or conduct meetings do so with heads properly covered in harmony with the Scriptural arrangement. (1 Cor. 11:3-16) In most cases, they remain seated, facing the group. None of the sisters give actual discourses at their meetings, but they read and comment on the material provided by the Watch Tower Society, or, for variety, they may cover it in discussion between two of them or as a demonstration. No counsel is given on their presentations in the Theocratic Ministry School, but by discussion they can benefit fully from the information that is normally covered on the school program.

If there are any persons in a newly formed congregation that qualify for appointment as elders or as ministerial servants, they will be recommended to the Society's branch office. This may be done by the body of elders of the congregation from which this newly formed group is dividing off, or, in the case of new congregations in isolated areas, it may be cared for during the visit of the circuit overseer. If there are none who qualify to be elders or ministerial servants, as in the case of a congregation made up entirely of sisters, the branch office will designate one of the group to care for correspondence with the office and to carry on meetings for the congregation. In time, when brothers qualify for appointment, they will care for these responsibilities.

TIME OF MEETINGS

The times at which the congregation meetings are held are determined locally. These may vary from place to place, because the matter is discussed with the congregation and then they choose times that are convenient for the majority of the members of the congregation.

KINGDOM HALL

The Kingdom Hall of Jehovah's Witnesses is the center of pure worship in the community. It is the principal location where meetings of the congregation are held, and it provides a central place from which the field ministry can be conducted.

In some communities a congregation may be small and so may meet in a private home. But just as soon as it proves to be both possible and practical, each congregation endeavors to obtain an adequate meeting hall. In some localities it is more convenient to rent a hall than to buy or to build. However, large numbers of congregations have chosen to purchase property and build their own Kingdom Hall, suited to their needs. It is up to all the dedicated members of the congregation to decide what they want to do in this matter.

If a congregation decides to build a Kingdom Hall, the body of elders usually designates as a building committee certain brothers who are very much interested in this particular construction work of the congregation and who may be good businessmen. This committee may or may not include the presiding overseer of the congregation, and it is not necessary to change the makeup of that building committee from year to year. They may take care of their duties as long as the committee is needed.

In connection with the ownership and operation of the Kingdom Hall it may be necessary to form an association. Sometimes it must be a legal corporation. Here, too, there is no need for change of officers from year to year.

Whether you own or rent your hall, it ought to be kept clean, both inside and out, so that it is a proper representation of Jehovah's true worship. A ministerial servant may be assigned to see that this work is cared for. Usually a schedule is worked out for the various congregation book study groups to take turns in cleaning the hall, along with a list of the things that need to be done each week. When your study group's turn comes, be sure to do your part.

There are a number of things that can be done to advertise the Kingdom Hall. For one thing, there should be a neat sign out in front bearing the words "Kingdom Hall of Jehovah's Witnesses" and an up-to-date listing of the times of meetings. If your hall has a window on street level, it is good to have an attractive display of literature so that passersby may observe. The display should be kept up-to-date and clean, using current literature and changing the arrangement from time to time. Some newspapers publish free notices of meeting times and special events, and the congregation may want to take advantage of this service. It may also be that the phone number of one of Jehovah's witnesses could beneficially be listed under "Jehovah's Witnesses."

Besides the above means of advertising, do not fail to make good use of any handbills and tracts provided by your congregation. Distribute them freely. They provide an excellent reminder to the people in your community that Jehovah's witnesses are active among them and are ready and willing to help them.

At every meeting in the Kingdom Hall there should be a brother, preferably a ministerial servant, who is an attendant. He may be assisted by other brothers, if necessary. He ought to have a friendly personality and be interested in meeting people who come to the hall and making them feel welcome. When he observes newcomers, he can get acquainted with them and may introduce them to others in the congregation, including some of the elders. He should offer his services to help latecomers to find seats and be alert to give any necessary attention to proper heating and ventilation in the hall. Also, if children cause a disturbance during the meeting, or run unrestrained before or after the meeting, it is his responsibility to see that the situation is given the needed attention.

In addition to its use for regular congregation meetings and as a meeting place for field service, the Kingdom Hall may be used for wedding ceremonies and funeral services and other spiritual functions, with the permission of the congregation's service committee.

CIRCUIT ASSEMBLIES

Everyone who regularly attends the meetings at the Kingdom Hall also looks forward with eager anticipation to the larger assemblies of Jehovah's people that are held periodically.

Twice a year a number of congregations that are served by the same circuit overseer meet together for a two-day assembly. Upbuilding talks and practical demonstrations are presented; counsel is given that is designed to meet the needs of that circuit. Such assemblies also afford opportunity for the baptism of new disciples.

The circuit assembly is usually held on a Saturday and a Sunday, though other days may be used if local circumstances make them preferable. Special programs arranged for the benefit of everyone are scheduled on Saturday and Sunday, and you are urged to be on hand to benefit from all of them. Arrangements may also be made for participation in the field service in the morning, generally on both days.

On Sunday morning at the assembly there is a meeting of the circuit and district overseers with the elders from the congregations in the circuit. At this meeting the district overseer presides as chairman. The shepherding work and the spiritual condition of the congregations are considered. Among other things, there may be a discussion of important material recently published by the "faithful and discreet slave," to be sure that all fully understand it and will be able to help those associated with the congregations to grasp it and to put it to work in their lives.

DISTRICT ASSEMBLIES

Other, larger assemblies are also held. Once a year a number of circuits usually gather for what is called a district assembly. At these district assemblies, and at the occasional national and international assemblies, some of the most thrilling discourses and announcements in the modern-day history of Jehovah's people have been presented.

Not only must those in attendance have their spiritual needs cared for through the program itself, but also their physical needs require attention. Sufficient rooming accommodations must be obtained. Usually the hotels do not have enough rooms for our large conventions; besides, many of the delegates who come as family groups are of moderate means, and they need something economical. Often the brothers in the assembly city arrange to accommodate conventioners in their homes. Also, house-to-house visits may be made to contact local residents who are willing to rent rooms at reasonable rates. Food is usually made available on the assembly grounds and is served to conventioners for a moderate price. Attendants are also required. These and many other services necessary to the operation of the assembly are performed by volunteer workers attending the assembly. None of them are paid for their work, but they willingly serve out of love for their Christian brothers.—Ps. 110:3.

By availing yourself of all these provisions to assemble with your Christian brothers, you will be protected against the spirit of the world, strengthened in faith and equipped to be a better servant of Jehovah God.—Phil. 4:8; Rom. 12:2.

CHAPTER 6

YOUR SERVICE TO GOD

SERVICE to God involves one's whole life. That is why the apostle Paul could say: "Whether you are eating or drinking or doing anything else, do all things for God's glory," and, "Whatever you are doing, work at it whole-souled as to Jehovah, and not to men, for you know that it is from Jehovah you will receive the due reward of the inheritance. Slave for the Master, Christ." —1 Cor. 10:31; Col. 3:23, 24.

For our service to be acceptable to God we must, indeed, submit to Christ as our Master. As he truthfully said: "I am the way and the truth and the life. No one comes to the Father except through me." (John 14:6) To him Jehovah has given "all authority" as King and Head of the Christian congregation. (Matt. 28:18) So, we must be Jesus' disciples, following his lead and obeying his commands, in order to be included among those whom Jehovah acknowledges as his servants.

THE CHRISTIAN'S MINISTRY

Have you personally responded to Jesus' invitation, "Take my yoke upon you and become my disciples," thereby finding refreshment for your soul? (Matt. 11: 28-30) That yoke of discipleship to Christ is a kindly one with a light load, especially so when compared with the yoke and load that people carry in the world and in their false religions. Nevertheless, a yoke implies service.

As disciples we must be like our teacher. (Luke 6:40) Jesus said that he came, 'not to be ministered to, but to minister.' (Matt. 20:28) To minister means to serve, particularly rendering service of a personal nature. (Luke 17:7, 8; Matt. 20:26, 27) Jesus was the minister *of God*, but he ministered *on behalf of* the people. (Luke 4:16-21) As his disciples, we are ministers of God and his Son, but we also minister on behalf of our fellow humans.

Are we married or do we have children? Then we have a divine obligation toward our mates and children. Husbands have the responsibility of headship. (Eph. 5:23, 28, 29; 6:1-4; Titus 2:4, 5) When we discharge our marital or parental obligations by ministering to the spiritual and material needs of those for whom God has made us responsible, we are rendering service as to God. But what if we were like persons of the world who discharge such obligations without a right motive, or in ways not conforming to God's will? Then this service would not be a Christian ministry. It would not be rendered in imitation of our Lord Jesus Christ.

Within congregations, some have the God-given responsibility to minister to God's flock, acting as overseers and ministerial servants. And men and women, individually, may voluntarily minister to the needs of their brothers and sisters. As their hearts move them to do so, they can encourage and aid fellow believers in whatever way they can, both spiritually and materially. (Rom. 15:25-27; 1 John 3:16-18) All this is part of the overall Christian ministry.

MINISTERING TO PERSONS
IN THE WORLD OF MANKIND

Here, however, we are primarily concerned with that part of our Christian ministry pertaining to those outside the congregation. Not all of us have mates, children or assigned responsibilities in congregations. But all true Christians share the privilege of publicly proclaiming the Kingdom good news. We see this in Jesus' parable of the sower. There Jesus showed that all who receive the "word of the kingdom" into their hearts should also bear fruit. (Matt. 13:18-23) What is that fruit? It must correspond with what is sown, namely, "the word [or, message] of the kingdom." So, the righteous-hearted ones produce as fruitage the "word of the kingdom" by speaking it out to others.

Jesus said, too, that some would produce 'a hundred-fold, some sixty, some thirty.' Grain sown in a field normally varies in production according to circumstances. Likewise, what persons can do in making proclamation of the good news will naturally vary according to each one's circumstances, and Jesus showed that he recognized this. Some have greater opportunity than others; some have greater health and vigor than others; some learn the truth earlier in life than others. Of course, each of us should want to be as productive of the "word of the kingdom" as we can. If it is truly done in a whole-souled way, Jehovah God and his Son are pleased with whatever one is able to do.

In another parable, Jesus said: "My Father is glorified in this, that you keep bearing much fruit and prove yourselves my disciples." In this parable the "fruit" is the overall Christian fruitage of fine works and evidence of God's spirit operating in our lives every day, but it must also include the bearing of the fruit of Kingdom proclamation.—John 15:2, 8; Matt. 7:16-20; Gal. 5:22, 23.

THE ANOINTED AND "OTHER SHEEP" SHARE IN MINISTERING

Those whom Christ personally commissioned to bear witness of him and to make disciples were men in line to become anointed members of spiritual Israel, in a new covenant with God. These, eventually totaling 144,000, would reign with him in his heavenly government. But while on earth, all of them were to serve as "ambassadors substituting for Christ," urging others to "become reconciled to God." (2 Cor. 5:20; Rev. 14:1, 3; Acts 1:8) Today only a remnant of such spirit-anointed ones remain on earth. However, associated with them now is a large number of other persons who have also become disciples of Christ Jesus, but who have the hope of living in a paradise earth as subjects of the heavenly government.—John 10:16.

These latter ones are the "sheep" in the parable at Matthew 25:31-46. They are persons who do good to Christ's brothers, the spirit-anointed ones, ministering to their needs because of recognizing their righteous service to God. Today such persons already form a "great crowd," as described at Revelation 7:9-17. They render God "sacred service day and night in his temple," and God favors them. They are not silent servants but "keep on crying with a loud voice, saying: 'Salvation we owe to our God, who is seated on the throne, and to the Lamb.'"

Any work that contributes to the advancement of Kingdom interests they willingly perform under the direction of the anointed Kingdom heirs. So, they are like the "Nethinim" of ancient times, who were not Israelites but served at God's temple, doing necessary work under the direction of the Levites.—Ezra 8:17, 20.

The rightness and importance of their sharing in bringing the truth to others is shown at Revelation 22:17, which says: "And the spirit and the bride [the spirit-anointed class] keep on saying: 'Come!' And let anyone hearing say: 'Come!' And let anyone thirsting come; let anyone that wishes take life's water free." Having heard the invitation from those of the bride class, the "great crowd" have the responsibility to extend that invitation to others who will hear. Like the anointed ones, they exercise faith in their hearts, and so with their mouths they make public declaration as ministers of God and of his Son. (Rom. 10:9, 10) Today these "other sheep" far outnumber the remnant and are doing the bulk of the Kingdom-preaching and disciple-making throughout the earth.

"BUYING OUT THE OPPORTUNE TIME"

To render sacred service to God in his temple or great spiritual arrangement for worship, we must heed the apostle Paul's exhortation: "Keep strict watch that how you walk is not as unwise but as wise persons, buying out the opportune time for yourselves, because the days are wicked. On this account cease becoming unreasonable, but go on perceiving what the will of Jehovah is." (Eph. 5:15-17) We 'buy out the opportune time' by not using it in the "unfruitful works that belong to the darkness," but by using it instead in fine works of Christian living and activity.—Eph. 5:10, 11, 18-20.

The question arises, then: How are we to apportion out our time so that our various obligations all receive proper attention? For example, how can we determine how much of our time to spend in Kingdom-preaching and disciple-making without neglecting the other features of our Christian ministry?

Husbands and fathers have, of course, a primary responsibility before God to care for their families, spiritually and materially. Fathers and mothers should be keenly interested in doing disciple-making among their own offspring so that their children may gain life everlasting. And all of us should seek to make known the Kingdom—and possibly to make disciples—among our relatives, either members of our immediate families or others. (Mark 5:19) When Andrew of Bethsaida learned the identity of the Messiah, the first one that he told about it was his brother Simon. (John 1:35-42) Later, when Simon Peter was sent to give a witness to Cornelius in Caesarea, he found that Cornelius had "called together his relatives and intimate friends," and they, too, accepted the truth. (Acts 10:24, 44) Yes, we should show heartfelt interest in our relatives' gaining God's protection, as did the woman Rahab. In faith, she gathered those of her family together with her so that when God caused the fall of the city of their residence, Jericho, their lives were spared. (Josh. 2:9-21; 6:22-25) Surely to see some of our own relatives become disciples would bring us especially great joy.

There are others toward whom we also have a responsibility. Galatians 6:10 says: "Really, then, as long as we have time favorable for it, let us work what is good toward all, but especially toward those related to us in the faith." This shows that we have a prior obligation toward those who are spiritually our brothers and sisters. We should want to contribute to their spiritual welfare and help them, as necessary, to continue as faithful disciples of Christ Jesus.

Still, we would not be true disciples of Christ Jesus if our loving concern did not reach out beyond our families, our close associates and our spiritual brothers. As Jesus put it: "If you love those loving you, what reward do you have? Are not also the tax collectors doing the same thing? And if you greet your brothers only, what extraordinary thing are you doing? Are not also the people of the nations doing the same thing? You must accordingly be perfect [or, whole, or, complete], as your heavenly Father is perfect." (Matt. 5:46-48)

Yes, we should show a full, rounded-out love that reaches out and embraces as many persons as it can. Such love should move us to set aside time, regularly if possible, to share the good news with others, though we may never personally have met them before.

Do we fully appreciate the grave danger that those outside God's congregation are in, their urgent need to learn of God's provisions for survival of the coming "great tribulation"? Putting ourselves in their place, are we moved to 'do for them what we would want done for ourselves,' namely, to aid them to gain the comforting and lifesaving truths of God's Word?—Matt. 7:12.

Over and above our desire to help others to gain salvation, there should be a keen interest on our part in sharing in the sanctification and the vindication of Jehovah's holy name. (Matt. 6:9) We love his name because it stands for him and all his wonderful qualities of goodness, loving-kindness, righteousness and justice. Knowing that his name has been falsely represented among the peoples of all the earth, our love for him should move us to do all we can to make the truth about him known everywhere.—Ps. 72:18, 19; Heb. 6:10.

METHODS USED BY JESUS AND HIS DISCIPLES

What methods should we use as we carry on this work of preaching and disciple-making? Since love is positive, we do not wait for persons to come to us or for them to ask to be helped. We should take the initiative and be resourceful, seeking ways to help them.

Christ Jesus set the example. He went to the people in their cities and villages. (Matt. 9:35; Luke 8:1) His work was of a very open and public nature. As a Jew, he could teach in the temple area or go into synagogues, speaking to large numbers. (John 18:20) People in that time commonly gathered in the marketplaces, the public squares by the city gates, even on principal streets, to discuss matters of public interest. There they learned the news of the day, and Jesus used these places to declare the best news. (Compare Proverbs 1:20, 21; 8: 1-3.) He talked to crowds on a mountainside or at the seashore. (Matt. 5:1, 2; 13:1, 2) Some persons received him into their homes, perhaps providing meals or lodging, and he rewarded them with personal instruction.

(Luke 10:38-42) Others would go to the home where he was staying, and he gladly taught them or performed other services for them.—Mark 2:1, 2; 10:10-16; Luke 19:5-10.

His disciples followed his zealous example, discharging their commission to bear witness about him to the ends of the earth, as he instructed following his resurrection. (Acts 1:8) They, too, talked to large groups in the temple area, in synagogues, marketplaces and other sites where people congregated. (Acts 5:12-16, 19-21, 25, 41, 42; 13:5, 14-16; 14:1; 16:13-15; 17:17-21) Paul taught daily in an auditorium in Ephesus. (Acts 19:8-10) Philip witnessed to an Ethiopian official while the man rode in his chariot.—Acts 8:26-40.

As can be seen, the preaching of Jesus and his disciples was largely to groups or even crowds. God's holy spirit did much to make this possible, causing large numbers to give attention and see the miraculous evidence of divine backing of these men. (Acts 2:1-6, 41, 43; 8:5-8; 9:40-42; 13:6-12) God's angels also shared, directing and supporting the disciples in their witness. (Acts 5:19-21; 8:26; 10:3-7, 22; 12:7-11) Christ Jesus personally supervised everything from his heavenly position at God's right hand. (Acts 2:32, 33; 9:3-6, 10-16; 16:6-10; 18:9-11) Thus, though the disciples put forth diligent and loving effort, they all recognized that what was accomplished was not by their own power or to their credit, as if they were anything in themselves. (1 Cor. 1:26-29; 2 Cor. 4:5) The increase in believers was from Jehovah.—Acts 2:47; 11:21; 14:27; 1 Cor. 3:5-9.

METHODS USED TODAY

Today Jehovah's Christian witnesses follow the same principles as did Christ Jesus and his early disciples. They too carry the good news to the people, instead of waiting for these to take the initiative. In some lands they can do much witnessing in public places, such as plazas and marketplaces, and find people willing to listen. However, in many parts of the earth circumstances today are different from those in the first century. People generally rely on newspapers, radio and television for news. Public discussion is relatively rare.

Thus, today the preaching of the good news has adapted itself to the broader circumstances that exist. Jesus said even to "preach from the housetops." Much of his counsel and instruction dealt with the disciples' attitude toward the people, their being free from fear in speaking the truth and having confidence in God's backing of them in their work. So, this allows freedom to adopt whatever witnessing methods prove to be effective and are in harmony with righteous principles. —Matt. 10:27, 28.

DECLARING THE GOOD NEWS TO PEOPLE IN THEIR HOMES

In lands where it is possible, Jehovah's Christian witnesses make an effort to visit all homes, going from one house to the next, even though no prior interest was shown. For over half a century now this has been the major means used to proclaim "this good news of the kingdom." Jesus said that "wisdom is proved righteous by its works," and the good results obtained show the wisdom of this method.—Matt. 11:19.

Going from house to house allows for personal aid to those met, affording opportunity for them to bring up questions and to express themselves freely. Today people are not so inclined to discuss religious subjects publicly away from their homes. So, talking to individuals or family groups in their homes is well suited to modern circumstances, as well as to our personal abilities.

At the same time, the effort put forth to reach people in this personal way, despite the fact that many reject the message, is evidence of our love for God and for our neighbor. Such visiting shows that our love is not partial, for we make an effort to give everyone an opportunity to hear the words of life.

What should we talk about when we call on people in this way? Our aim is to bring understanding and appreciation of the Bible. Jesus' preaching and that of his disciples regularly focused on the Scriptures. (John 7:16-18; Acts 17:2; 18:28) So it is good to have one or more Scripture texts in mind that you could read and discuss. Since most persons we visit have relatively little understanding of God's Word, our presentation needs to be one that will be easily grasped.

Jesus' preaching and that of his disciples centered around the Kingdom, so we, too, point to it as the real remedy for mankind's ills and the means for carrying out God's will. (Matt. 4:17; Acts 19:8; 28:23) Also, by his entire life course, Jesus sanctified the name of Jehovah. We should do the same, honoring that name and aiding others to appreciate its significance as we do. —John 17:6; Isa. 43:10-12.

Aside from these major points, what you say at any one home will generally depend on the response of the one visited. You are free to discuss what appears to be best for aiding each individual. There are no detailed rules as to how you should begin conversations or how to answer questions. Sincere interest in the persons to whom you talk is the key to reaching the hearts of righteously disposed ones. Fill your mind and heart with Bible truth and look to Jehovah God and his Son to direct you through the power of the holy spirit. Of the woman Lydia, the record says that "Jehovah opened her heart wide to pay attention to the things being spoken by Paul." (Acts 16:14) He can do the same with individuals to whom we speak today.

Of course, there is much that you can learn from other Witnesses, from their good example and their experiences. You can also learn from your own successes and mistakes. And, most of all, you will want to learn from Bible examples and counsel.

When you approach people in their homes, do so without fear that more is expected of you by God or by the congregation than you can give. Be confident that kindness, consideration and unselfish interest, coupled with firm faith and conviction that what you present is God's message, will always accomplish the most good. But also realize that the majority will not accept the truth when they first hear it. Yet we can rejoice that, in God's mercy, he often grants persons many opportunities to hear, with the result that some eventually do believe. Some persons on whom you call will be genuinely busy with matters that, at least to them, seem urgent. So you may find that you are able to make only a few brief remarks. But your being considerate may well bring a warmer response the next time a Witness calls. Genuine love is not impatient or harsh but is "long-suffering and kind."—1 Cor. 13:4.

People in some lands are prejudiced against Christianity or are ignorant of it and perhaps of the Bible itself. One may have to appeal to reason and logic to persuade them of the truth of the Scriptures, even as the apostles did. (Acts 9:22; 17:2, 18-31) Jehovah will help us as he helped them.

Some persons are not religiously inclined, and we may find it best simply to quote the scriptures or paraphrase these for them rather than to read directly from the Bible. But others will be happy for us to show them the texts in our Bible, or, better yet, in their own copy, and they will be impressed by seeing for themselves what God's Word says. (Compare Acts 17:11, 12.) So, we can endeavor to be like the apostle Paul and "become all things to people of all sorts," that we might somehow serve as instruments of God for their salvation.—1 Cor. 9:19-23.

USE OF LITERATURE

Another method used effectively to spread the good news in our day is distribution of printed literature. In this way the Bible itself has been made available to vast portions of earth's population. Additionally, books, booklets, magazines and tracts explaining the Bible have been of tremendous help in reaching out into "all the inhabited earth" with the Kingdom message in all the principal languages. Much more has been accomplished than would ever have been possible if the work of preaching and disciple-making had been limited to explanation by word of mouth.

Although a person may seem to show very little interest when approached by a proclaimer of the good news, if literature is left with him he may read it and thus benefit from the more extended witness that it gives. Or that piece of literature may be picked up by another member of the household or a visitor, one who is really searching for the truth. Further, with literature, those who are interested can make rapid progress in gaining knowledge without your having to spend the time that would be required to explain every point verbally.

The Society's branch offices generally suggest through the monthly pamphlet the *Kingdom Ministry* the publications to be featured during certain periods. This helps to facilitate printing and shipping. It is thus possible for the printing establishments of the Watch Tower Society and associated corporations to coordinate their operations with greater effectiveness as they endeavor to supply the needs of you and your brothers. This does not mean, of course, that only the designated literature may be used during any certain period. Where it appears evident to you that the person to whom you are witnessing would particularly benefit from a certain publication, you are always free to offer it to him.

Magazines have a special appeal for many persons. They are current, have articles on a variety of subjects and can be read in a relatively short time. They can help us to reach persons who show only limited interest. *The Watchtower* especially aids them in gaining vital Bible knowledge. Each issue contains articles that are designed to be specially appealing to the public, as well as material for more advanced Bible students. *Awake!* can also stimulate their appreciation for God's Word, as it aids them to see life as it really is and tactfully underlines their need for Bible counsel and guidance.

Every week or so these periodicals provide us something new to offer. Because of the fine results already obtained from doing so, many of Jehovah's witnesses regularly set aside time to call at homes to offer just these magazines. They have found it effective simply to make a very brief presentation of the magazines and thus visit many homes in a relatively short time. In offering the magazines, they may draw attention to some article that they believe is likely to appeal to the householder and then offer the magazines for the regular contribution. In this manner they have a fine share in giving a witness to the Kingdom, keeping it prominently before the minds of the people.

The magazines may be offered at any appropriate time or place. Some Witnesses have good results in offering them to fellow employees where they work, to persons who call at their home, to those whom they meet when traveling or shopping. Others make brief calls with the magazines at business places or they approach people on the street in shopping areas.

Often you will find persons who express appreciation for the *Watchtower* and *Awake!* magazines. They are pleased to obtain them whenever you call. Some Witnesses have a regular route of persons to whom they carry these faith-strengthening magazines. You may want to do that too. And, as has frequently happened, these regular visits may open the way for further Bible discussions during which you may be able to help them really to know and love our grand God, Jehovah, and his Son Jesus Christ.

TERRITORY IN WHICH TO PREACH AND TEACH

As an aid toward orderly accomplishment of the work, congregations, as well as individuals who do Kingdom-preaching in isolated areas, receive assignments of territory, both city and rural areas, from the branch offices directing the work in their respective lands. This finds some precedent in the God-directed arrangement existing among certain of the apostles in the first century. (2 Cor. 10:13; Gal. 2:9) It avoids much overlapping of effort and contributes toward thorough visitation, giving as many as possible the opportunity to hear.

If you so desire, you may approach the one who supervises the assigning of territory in your congregation and request any portion of such territory that has not already been assigned out. Then, each time that you cover the territory, it is requested that you inform him of that. For convenience and best use of the time you may wish to have a territory near your home. Having such a personal territory enables you to get to know many persons, and, with patience, you may have the joy of aiding some of them to come to appreciate God's provision for salvation.

Of course, you will want to get in touch with just as many of the people who live in the territory as possible. But, as you make your calls, you will probably find that some are not at home. What can be done? A tract or a magazine may be left in the door, preferably out of view of passersby. It is also helpful to keep a written record of those houses. Then, if possible, call back on a different day of the week or at a different time of day. Some have found it good to call later on the telephone where possible, or to write a brief letter, mentioning their efforts and explaining the purpose of their visit, perhaps including a piece of literature. In some cases, Witnesses have considerately invited certain physically infirm ones in the congregation to do such telephoning or letter writing for them so that these may have a wider share in the Kingdom-preaching.

Similar methods may be used to reach the occupants of apartments that are not readily accessible. Or perhaps the doorman will accept tracts or handbills for distribution to the occupants. Business places in your territory may also be visited at convenient times, and often the owner or manager will grant you permission to speak very briefly to the employees.

The arrangement of working in territory that has been assigned to us by the local congregation will avoid confusion in our activity as well as irritation on the part of householders due to simultaneous coverage of the same area by two or more Witnesses. By cooperating we show consideration both for our brothers and for the people in the territory.

GROUP WITNESSING

Many of our brothers and sisters, and particularly those newly sharing in the Kingdom-preaching, find it very encouraging and helpful to do group witnessing. We know that Jesus sent his disciples out in pairs to the cities and villages where they would preach.—Mark 6:7; Luke 10:1.

Often those sharing together in group activity attend the same congregation book study and live in the same general area. Where this is so, the book study conductor can obtain the needed territory for the group. Efforts should be made to arrange things as conveniently as possible for them. Often more than one weekly arrangement can be made, some being able to share on weekends, some on certain weekdays, or perhaps on certain evenings.

The place of the group's meeting for witnessing may be where the congregation book study is held or some other location, according to what is convenient and what Christian considerateness for home conditions makes advisable.

Similarly, as to times for beginning Kingdom-preaching activity, local circumstances merit consideration. Some areas may allow for earlier visitation than others. The desire to devote as much time as possible in preaching should be balanced with good judgment as to what will be most likely to bring a favorable response on the part of the people being visited.

When sharing in group witnessing, your being on time will be appreciated by all. And, since there are usually a preliminary discussion of the day's text and other helpful comments or suggestions before going to the territory, it will ensure your not missing out on these. By being present you will also benefit from the prayer for God's direction and help offered at the close of this ten- or fifteen-minute discussion. Where meeting for evening activity, the discussion may be more limited, though appropriately including a prayer.

In assigning sections of territory in which to witness, the one taking the lead will usually try to provide each one with sufficient territory to last the entire period of that day's activity, thus avoiding unnecessary waiting and loss of time. Some may plan to spend part of the time in calling back on interested ones or conducting studies, and it is good for the one taking the lead to find this out and to help all to coordinate their activity to the extent he can. (1 Cor. 14:40) Following such group activity, be sure to let the one taking the lead know how much of the territory assigned to you was visited, as it would be fine to give each territory a thorough coverage before it is turned in.

As an "association of brothers" we all want to help one another. (1 Pet. 2:17) If you would like assistance in your preaching and teaching work, feel free to speak to any of the congregation elders or to the one conducting the congregation book study that you attend. In time, as you grow in ability and confidence, it may be your privilege to aid other newer ones to make progress, and you will find this a real joy.

It is our desire to bring the good news to as many as possible in the yet remaining time. So it is usually more advantageous for the Kingdom proclaimers to visit homes singly, even though close together. Circumstances determine, however, and particularly in dangerous areas it may be advisable to go two by two, especially at night. Then, too, in some areas a married couple may obtain better response by calling together at homes. In all cases, good judgment coupled with our sincere concern to accomplish the most possible should govern the arrangements we make.

MAKING DISCIPLES BY RETURN VISITS
AND HOME BIBLE STUDIES

The commission given to God's anointed ones, and which commission the "other sheep" help them to carry out, is not only to preach the good news for the purpose of a witness but also to make disciples. (Matt. 24:14; 28:19, 20) You can contribute to the fulfillment of this commission by following up on all who show interest as a result of your personal efforts to make the truth known.

Such persons may take some literature; or their interest may be manifest in other ways, in comments they make. It may simply be that you see evidence of a right heart condition that causes you to believe that further efforts in talking to the person might bring fruitful results. If at all possible, revisit such ones yourself and aid them to gain further knowledge. If you are not able to do so, or have reason to believe that the individual would be more receptive to someone else, then endeavor to have another Witness call to further the person's interest in the truth. To do this, of course, you will need to note down the names and addresses of all those showing interest.

As with Christians in the first century, it is a cause for great joy to all of us when we see or hear of persons converting to true worship. We know that this means life for them and that it magnifies Jehovah's greatness and goodness. (Acts 11:18; 15:3) If we fully appreciate that our aim is to aid righteously disposed persons to gain life, and that all the various preaching activities and the different literature employed are means to that end, then we will do our best to follow up interest shown.

Since lives are at stake and we live in times of great urgency, we will want to return to visit such ones, or see that they are visited, at the very first opportunity. Careful thought and good planning of our activity, rather than leaving matters to chance, will enable us to give the needed help in time.

In order to understand the Bible's message, what God's purposes are and what they must do to gain his favor and life, most persons need to have many questions answered and much explanation given. In modern times, the most effective means found to accomplish this has been that of home Bible studies, using publications provided by the "faithful and discreet slave" class through the Watch Tower Society. This systematic coverage of Bible truths makes possible steady progress. The vast majority of those today associated with Jehovah's people earth wide were helped by such a home Bible study.

Many have good success in offering a home Bible study on initial calls while visiting from door to door. In other cases, such studies can be established by calling back on those who have shown some interest. In either case, it has proved effective to demonstrate the study method used by Jehovah's witnesses, considering one or two paragraphs from one of the Watch Tower publications. However, before demonstrating the home Bible study arrangement it may be necessary to converse with the person for awhile, perhaps answering some questions. With some persons, several visits may be required before a study can be started. When people see how the Bible answers questions that have concerned them, this is usually what succeeds in interesting them in having a home Bible study on a regular basis.

There is no arbitrary ruling as to how the study should be conducted, but be sure that the student really understands the points discussed. We recommend that you urge the student to study the lesson before you come, and you may even find it beneficial to demonstrate how to do this. In this way it will be possible to ask the questions on the paragraphs, look up the scriptures that are cited, and then read the material in the paragraphs as a summary. When the study is new, you may find it beneficial to look up all the scriptures, even though some are quoted directly in the publication. In this way you focus principal attention on the Bible itself. But after a short time, it should be possible simply to discuss what the texts quoted in the paragraphs say, while looking up those that are cited but not quoted. This will enable you to make greater headway. You will undoubtedly seek Jehovah's blessing regularly before you go to conduct the study. As to the student, however, you will have to determine when he is properly adjusted religiously to show him the importance of prayer to Jehovah through Christ in connection with the study. Then it would be appropriate to open your study each week with prayer, asking Jehovah's blessing, and to conclude with a prayer of thanksgiving for the fine things learned. —Ps. 25:4; Jas. 1:5; Eph. 5:20.

In our discipling work we may well follow the example of the apostle Paul, who had a prominent share in making disciples. From what we read of the way he served brothers in the congregations, we can be sure that he did not teach new disciples in such a way as to draw attention to himself or to cause others to look up to him as their leader. (1 Cor. 1:13-15; 2:1-5; 3:5-7; Matt. 23:10) He always directed attention to Jehovah God and to his Son Jesus Christ, the appointed Head of the Christian congregation. In harmony with God's declared will, Paul 'laid Christ as a foundation' by teaching the truth about him, including the truth concerning Christ's ransom sacrifice, aiding others to make belief in that truth part of their own lives. Furthermore, he stressed that any building done on that foundation ought to be of fire-resistant materials, with characteristics like those of gold, silver and precious stones. That is, durable Christian qualities had to be built into the individual being instructed in God's Word, otherwise all that spiritual building work would be destroyed when subjected to fiery trial. (1 Cor. 3:10-15) Surely no one would want that to happen to his work.

Those same principles of building that applied to the discipling work done by Paul and his associates in connection with prospective members of the body of Christ also apply to the discipling work in which you are privileged to share today. Those that you teach need more than to be able to answer certain questions on basic doctrinal matters. Rather, as Paul wrote to those whom he had taught: "You should be made new in the force actuating your mind, and should put on the new personality which was created according to God's will in true righteousness and loyalty." (Eph. 4:23, 24) Gaining accurate knowledge is a necessary part of putting on this new personality with its many durable qualities. The needed changes just do not take place when a person does not understand a matter clearly. So, patiently explain matters to those with whom you study and draw them out occasionally with questions to be sure they understand.—Col. 3:10.

As you study with them, help them to see the Scriptural reasons for things that are said. Encourage them to incorporate scriptures in their answers and to seek out Bible principles when decisions must be made. In this way inculcate deep regard for Scriptural principles and reliance on Jehovah God.—Prov. 3:5-7.

To make real progress, of course, the truth must affect a person's heart. So, pause at appropriate points to build appreciation. In that way you build up the hearts of the ones with whom you are studying. (Prov. 4:23) As opportunity affords, highlight the grand qualities of Jehovah God as manifest in his works and purposes, so helping the students to draw closer to God. Inculcate deep respect for Jehovah's wisdom so that they will readily respond to the direction of his Word. Magnify his justice, helping to fortify them against the onslaughts of skeptics. Help them to know Jehovah as one who loves his servants and cares for them and to whom they can turn with confidence. (1 John 4:10) In this way work toward developing in them a strong feeling of devotion and loyalty toward Jehovah, and a desire to please him in everything that they do. Aid them to appreciate God's Son, Christ Jesus, in similar ways. If they truly know Jehovah and his Son and love God's ways, they will never forsake the service of Jehovah or become indifferent about his will for them.—1 Chron. 28:9; John 17:3.

Something else that they need to be taught is appreciation for the congregation arrangement under the headship of Christ Jesus. Over a period of time, help them to appreciate the importance of unity of worship and action among all God's people earth wide. Show them that an orderly arrangement was instituted by Christ Jesus among the disciples in the Christian congregation in the first century and that this same arrangement prevails today under his continuing headship.

As soon as it seems appropriate, invite the newly interested ones to go along with you to the congregation meetings. When they accept such invitation, you can help them to feel welcome at the Kingdom Hall, introducing them to some of the congregation elders and others.

As you study together week after week, keep in mind

that for these persons to gain life they must eventually begin to bring forth fruit, the "word of the kingdom." So they need to be helped to think in terms of using what they learn. You can explain to them some points about Kingdom-preaching and disciple-making and show what a privilege it is to share in this. They may start by sharing things learned with relatives, friends and others. Gradually their desire to have a fuller share in this grand privilege of service will grow, and, when they qualify, it can be your happy privilege to help them get started in the public ministry.

It is, of course, necessary to maintain a balance in doing these many things at home Bible studies. While endeavoring to accomplish the things suggested, at each home Bible study we also want to cover a reasonable amount of material in the publication used. It is good to draw the student out occasionally with additional questions, but this should not be overdone. One cannot hope that the student will get all the many aspects of any one Bible doctrine right away. Concentrate on the essential points in the paragraph or scriptures involved. If we can lay a solid groundwork, the students will be able to learn some of the finer points of the matter as they continue on in Christian discipleship. By making reasonable and steady progress the person will also get a feeling of advancing, of getting an ever-growing picture of God's purpose. This will be encouraging.

In determining how long to continue studying with a person, you must consider the circumstances. After a time the person's sincerity or depth of interest in serving God should become apparent. If, after a sufficient number of studies, the person does not manifest any real progress, then it may be that you could spend the time more beneficially on other calls.

On the other hand, if the person gives evidence of appreciation of the things being learned, and shows some measure of progress, you will want to continue to help him to grow in knowledge, in love and in appreciation of the privilege of serving Jehovah God. Even after persons begin sharing in the Kingdom-preaching or take the step of baptism, it is usually advisable to continue studying with them for a time until they get well established in the way of the truth.

REPORTING OUR FIELD ACTIVITY

As a matter of interest, Jehovah's witnesses of modern times report their activity in Kingdom-preaching and disciple-making to their local congregations. Each congregation, in turn, compiles a report of the activity of all its members and forwards this to the branch office. Some individuals who are engaged in special ministries also report directly to the branch office. Then the branch office sends in a monthly report to the central office of the Watch Tower Society.

The record kept of the activity month by month and year by year enables us all to see the general progress of the preaching and discipling work. We are encouraged when we learn of increases by means of such reports. So, it is appreciated if all cooperate in making possible such report. A supply of report slips is available at the Kingdom Hall and it is requested that each one sharing in the preaching work turn in a report toward the close of each month, totaling thereon his or her personal witnessing activity during that month. The information that would be appreciated on these slips is as follows:

"Books," "Booklets," "Individual Magazines," and "New Subscriptions": The columns with these headings are for listing the total number of any of these items that you placed with persons who are not dedicated, baptized Witnesses.

"Hours in Field Service": Time spent in the activity of Kingdom-preaching and disciple-making, proclaiming God's truths to those who are not dedicated, baptized Witnesses. It does not matter what method is used, witnessing to people in their homes or to those coming to your own home, witnessing by letters, telephone or any other method. It would be productive of good results if each publisher endeavored to put in several hours each week in this direct witnessing. The time should be counted from when you personally begin such witnessing activity until its close. Those giving public talks may also count the time spent delivering these.

"Return Visits": The total number of return calls made on persons who are not dedicated, baptized Witnesses for the purpose of further stimulating interest previously shown. The return "visit" could be, not only by a visit to someone's home, but also in the form of a letter, a telephone call or the delivery of some literature, such as the latest issue of a magazine. Each time a home Bible study is conducted it should be counted as a return visit.

"Bible Studies": The total number of different Bible studies you conducted during the month (not the number of times each study was conducted) with persons who are not dedicated, baptized Witnesses and for which studies you are turning in a Bible Study Report.

In addition to your Field Service Report slip, it would be appreciated if, at the end of each month, you would fill out a Bible Study Report slip for each Bible study you conduct. When beginning a new study it would be best to conduct the study at least three times before reporting it, since, due to lack of interest, some persons discontinue their studies after the first or second time.

The congregation keeps a Publisher's Record card for each one sharing in the Kingdom proclamation, and your field service is recorded on it. If you should move to another congregation, it would be helpful to that congregation if you would ask the presiding overseer of the congregation where you have been associating to give you from the congregation files the Publisher's Record card bearing your name. This can be turned over to the presiding overseer of the congregation to which you move. When you are simply going to be away for awhile on a visit, it is better to mail your reports back to your home congregation, unless the visit is for a period of more than three months. Then it is requested that you take the Publisher's Record card with you to the congregation with which you will be associating.

PROPER VIEW OF REPORTS

As noted, service reports can provide a measure of encouragement due to seeing the progress of the discipling work around the earth. They may also serve as somewhat of a guide to the congregation elders as to what they might do to aid those desiring to have a full share in the proclamation of the good news.

However, we must realize that one can never put down on a report slip all the things that go into the Christian ministry—for this involves our whole life, not merely our preaching and teaching among those in the world of mankind. This report does not include all the vital preaching and teaching that goes on within the congregation, or, for that matter, all that we do to help our families.

Then, too, it is impossible to put into figures one's love, faith, kindness, devotion and all the other fruits of God's spirit, which really determine whether we will gain life everlasting. It is equally impossible to put into figures one's individual circumstances in life. It may take great effort, real determination, careful planning and considerable sacrifice for certain ones to spend some time each week in Kingdom-preaching. So, we should look upon such reports simply as information that is helpful, and often very encouraging when combined with those of the others in our congregation, in our country or earth wide.

We can be both comforted and stimulated, then, by keeping in mind the apostle's words when he says: "Consequently, my beloved brothers, become steadfast, unmovable, always having plenty to do in the work of the Lord, knowing that your labor is not in vain in connection with the Lord." (1 Cor. 15:58) We want to be a cleansed people, 'peculiarly God's own, zealous for fine works,' 'keeping our minds on maintaining fine works.' (Titus 2:14; 3:8) These fine works include both our ministering to one another within the congregation and our carrying the word of life to those outside.

WHO MAY SHARE WITH US IN OUR KINGDOM-PREACHING AND TEACHING?

Anyone, of course, is free to talk to others about God's Word. But some persons may do this who have not 'repented and turned around' from a course contrary to God's will and righteous standards. It could hardly be pleasing to God if the congregation were to recognize such as its approved associates.

However, some persons who have not yet been baptized may wish to share in public Kingdom-preaching with us. In fact, most persons who get baptized have already shared in such preaching activity. But before such persons accompany us in this public activity (or turn in reports) and thereby receive our recognition as approved associates, we should be satisfied that this will bring no reproach on the congregation and will not be displeasing to God. To determine this we should consider these points:

Do the person's expressions show that he believes the Bible is the inspired Word of God? (2 Tim. 3:16) Does he know and believe at least the basic teachings of the Scriptures so that, when asked questions, he will answer in harmony with the Bible, and not according to false religious teachings? (2 Tim. 2:15; Matt. 7:21-23) Is he heeding the Bible's command to associate with Jehovah's people in congregation meetings (if he physically and circumstantially can)? (Heb. 10:24, 25; Ps. 122:1) Does he apply in his life what the Bible says about honesty? (Eph. 4:25, 28) Does he know what the Bible says about fornication, adultery, polygamy and homosexuality, and does he live in harmony with it? If the person is living with one of the opposite sex, is the marriage legally registered? (Heb. 13:4; Matt. 19:9; 1 Cor. 6:9, 10; 1 Tim. 3:2, 12) Does he heed the Bible's prohibition of drunkenness? (Eph. 5:18; 1 Pet. 4:3, 4) Has he definitely broken off membership in all false religious organizations with which he may have been affiliated, and has he ceased attending their meetings and sharing in their activities? (Rev. 18:4; 2 Cor. 6:14-18) Is he free from any involvement in the political affairs of the world? (John 6:15; 15:19; Jas. 1:27) Does he believe and live in harmony with what the Bible, at Isaiah 2:4, says about the affairs of the nations? Does he want to be one of Jehovah's Christian witnesses?—Ps. 110:3.

Before inviting anyone to share with us in Kingdom-preaching, it would be wise to make sure that he understands these Scriptural requirements. If you have been conducting a Bible study with him for some time, you may know the answer to some of these questions already, due to his expressions. As to the others, you may look up the scriptures with him and get his expressions on them, making sure that he sees the import of what they say and that he understands that those who share with Jehovah's witnesses in their activity must be leading lives that harmonize with these Scriptural requirements. We are not seeking to have people share with us in our activity simply for the sake of large numbers. Our interest is in bringing praise to Jehovah God. To do that we must hold to standards of righteousness as a body of Christians. So, while we need not pry into a person's private life, we should be satisfied that those who begin to participate in the field ministry know what is expected of them and have the opportunity to indicate whether they feel they qualify or not.

Where persons do meet these requirements, they are welcome to share with us in Kingdom-preaching, and reports will also be accepted from them. Young children may wish to do so and, of course, their parents should supervise this. Where the children's motive is that of a desire to please God and help others to learn of him, this is a fine expression for them to make and they should be encouraged to manifest love of God and neighbor in this way. By word and their own example, the parents should concentrate on building up the child's love and appreciation of his Creator so that the child will *want* to share. The parents may require their children to accompany them when the parents themselves engage in such activity. But for the child to be viewed as a proclaimer of the good news, he must give a personal expression and his heart should be motivating him to do so. (Luke 6:45; Rom. 10:10) Only when this is the case should reports be accepted from such a child.

REASONS FOR JOYFUL CONFIDENCE

As we individually and collectively give attention to the urgent work of Kingdom-preaching and disciple-making, we have every reason for joyful confidence. Even as in the first century, it is not humans but Jehovah God and his Son Christ Jesus and the invisible angelic forces that do the major work, and we serve humbly and willingly as instruments. We need not be unduly anxious as to personal abilities. As long as we are sincerely striving to make progress in our service to God, he can make up for our lack. (1 Tim. 4:15) We do not need training in some theological institution of this world to qualify us as his servants, even as Jesus and his apostles did not need this.—John 7:14-17; Acts 4:13.

We may also remember that, while God's will is "that all sorts of men should be saved and come to an accurate knowledge of truth," he does not give us the assignment of converting the whole world of mankind. (1 Tim. 2:4) His Word shows that there is a dividing work going on among mankind. (Matt. 25:31-46) This good news is being preached "for a witness to all the nations" before the end of this system of things comes. (Matt. 24:14) We cannot make the people accept the truth, but we can help those who are "rightly disposed for everlasting life" to become disciples. (Acts 13:48) When Paul met persons who willfully resisted his sincere efforts to aid them, he turned away to find those who would be more receptive. We can do that too. Like him, we want to give all persons possible the opportunity and in this way no bloodguilt will rest upon us if any suffer destruction.—Acts 18:5-11; compare Ezekiel 2:7; 3:17-21.

As among the early Christians, so today gifts and abilities differ. (1 Cor. 12:4-31) Some may be quite effective in Kingdom-preaching, but not as effective in teaching and disciple-making. Some may be very good at initiating conversations with acquaintances, workmates, traveling companions, and so forth, while others may find they get their best results in the door-to-door activity. Even as within the congregation, so also in our activity outside, we want to serve in harmony with the apostle's exhortation at 1 Peter 4:10: "In proportion as each one has received a gift, use it in ministering to one another as fine stewards of God's undeserved kindness expressed in various ways." Yes, whatever our abilities, let us be whole-souled in what we do, serving Jehovah with our whole heart, mind and strength. —Luke 10:27.

As world conditions worsen, the carrying out of the Kingdom-preaching and disciple-making may call for increased ingenuity and resourcefulness on our part to reach people with the good news. Even as is the case today in some lands where bans are imposed, the proclaimers of the good news may need to use methods that do not attract public attention. The Bible allows for our doing so. Since Jesus Christ and his apostles gave only basic instructions as to the *way* in which this activity is to be carried on, this allows us the freedom to use whatever method is best under the circumstances, always adhering, of course, to Bible standards of righteousness and maintaining integrity to its moral precepts.

We must never lose from sight the fact that the effectiveness of the words we speak depends in large measure upon our living in accord with what we say. When Jehovah called upon the nation of Israel to serve as his witnesses, they were not then engaged in preaching to the nations or in making disciples. How, then, were they to serve as his witnesses? By giving living proof that their trust was undeniably fixed on Jehovah for protection and salvation and that their hope for all present and future blessings and happiness rested in him—not in men, nations, idol gods or material things. —Isa. 43:1-4, 10-13.

We, too, should give force to our verbal witness by demonstrating that our lives are lived in genuine faith, looking to God and his Son as the ones to bring us the desires of our heart in a righteous new order, not trusting in this present decaying system of things. Living according to the high standards of God's Word in our daily lives, our family affairs, our secular jobs, and our congregational activity, we will never be causing any hindrance that might deter others from accepting the good news we proclaim. Instead, we will be providing them with the evidence that God's Word, genuinely practiced, does indeed produce fine fruitage. So doing, we can "adorn the teaching of our Savior, God, in all things," enhancing and making very attractive such teaching.—Titus 2:10.

CHAPTER 7

SERVING JEHOVAH WHOLE-SOULED

THE greatest commandment of the Law, as quoted by Christ Jesus, requires whole-souled service: "You must love Jehovah your God with your whole heart and with your whole soul and with your whole mind and with your whole strength." (Mark 12:30) No less is required of us as disciples of Christ Jesus.

Serving Jehovah in this manner is not burdensome. (1 John 5:3) It is the normal thing for every person who truly appreciates his proper relationship to God.

Such service involves every fiber of one's very being, the entire person. The full motivation and desire of the heart should be to please Jehovah. One's full mental capacity and physical strength should be expended in doing the divine will. We do this, not because of compulsion from any human source, but because we are grateful to God through Christ Jesus for the undeserved kindness that they have shown to us.—2 Cor. 5:14, 15; 6:1, 2.

An outstanding example of one who rendered such whole-souled service to Jehovah as a disciple of Christ Jesus is the apostle Paul. In view of his former record as a persecutor of Christ's followers, Paul was especially grateful for having become a recipient of Jehovah's undeserved kindness. He expressed that appreciation by laboring in the service of God in excess of all the other apostles. (1 Cor. 15:9, 10) He traveled thousands of miles on land and by sea, establishing many congregations in Europe and Asia Minor. His journeys involved physical hardship. His zeal in declaring God's message of truth subjected him to persecution in the form of imprisonment, beating and even stoning. He also had to contend with the treachery of false brothers. Though he had the right to receive material support from the brothers, he chose to work with his hands in order not to impose an expensive burden on them. But as he said to elders of the congregation of Ephesus: "I do not make my soul of any account as dear to me, if only I may finish my course and the ministry that I received of the Lord Jesus, to bear thorough witness to the good news of the undeserved kindness of God." —Acts 20:24, 33-35; 2 Cor. 11:23-27; 1 Thess. 2:8, 9.

The fact that Paul labored in excess of other Christians did not make them inferior to him. Whole-souled service was required of them too. But Paul's circumstances were such that Jehovah God and his Son Jesus Christ were able to use him in a more extensive way. As a single man, Paul was not encumbered by family obligations. He also had a measure of health and stamina that enabled him to endure great hardship. But he humbly acknowledged the source of his real strength, saying: "For all things I have the strength by virtue of him who imparts power to me."—Phil. 4:13.

Your circumstances may well differ from those of Paul, so the service that you are able to perform will not be identical to his. But, just as he imitated Christ, his example is one that you can beneficially imitate. In what way? In willingness to put the lasting welfare of other people ahead of your own convenience, doing all things for God's glory.—1 Cor. 10:31–11:1.

It is to be expected that, following our baptism as disciples of Christ Jesus, our appreciation of Jehovah's undeserved kindness would grow and we would seek ways to express that appreciation more fully. Has that been true in your case? Are you applying the principles of God's Word more fully in all the various activities of your life? Has your love for fellow Christians widened out, and has that love come to be the kind that puts their interests ahead of your own, thus imitating the love that Jesus showed? Do you give less prominence to material things, so that you can share fully in the work of preaching and disciple-making? Has your love for Jehovah really grown to such an extent that you express it with "your whole heart and with your whole soul and with your whole mind and with your whole strength"? That should come to be true of each one of us.

When we were first learning the truth from God's Word, love for Jehovah and for Christ Jesus moved us to make major adjustments in our lives. Now, as we grow in appreciation of our relationship with our heavenly Father and of what his Son did on our behalf, are there other adjustments that we can make in order to be used more fully by him? As we ponder that question, it is helpful to review some of the fields of activity that are open to Jehovah's people.

SERVING WHERE THE NEED IS GREATER

No matter where a person lives, there is work to be done in Jehovah's service. But in some areas brothers are very much needed to assist in caring for interested persons and handling congregational responsibilities. Perhaps you are living in a city where publishers and pioneers are in a good position to study with interested persons in frequently covered territory and where enough brothers are available to provide shepherding and teaching for those associated with the congregation. In that case, if your circumstances permit it, you may wish to consider making yourself available for service in another location.

The value of such moves by capable brothers was appreciated even in the early days of the Christian congregation. When, for example, the Jerusalem congregation heard about the many persons who were becoming believers in Syrian Antioch, they sent Barnabas there to assist. Response was so outstanding that Barnabas went to Tarsus to invite Paul to help him. Paul accepted that invitation and, with Barnabas, labored for a whole year in building up the Antioch congregation spiritually.—Acts 11:22-26.

Perhaps you, like Barnabas and Paul, can make yourself available for work in a very productive field. Some individuals and family groups have been able to do so in a temporary way, devoting full weekends during the summer months to preaching in territories where people have only limited opportunities to hear the Kingdom message. Others have arranged their affairs to spend vacation time in such territories, using a portion of each day for the field ministry. Still others have moved into these areas to live, so that they can advance Kingdom interests there.

If it is your desire to serve in such a territory where your assistance can be used to good advantage, write to the branch office for suggestions on locations. Include such information as the name of your congregation, your age, date of baptism, whether you are serving as an elder or a ministerial servant in the congregation and whether you are married and have a family. If you have in mind a particular section of the country, be sure to mention this in your letter. If your desire is to move to another country with a view to sharing to the full in advancing Kingdom interests there, write directly to the branch office responsible for the territory in which you are interested. Such a move requires careful planning and strong reliance on Jehovah; it can also bring rich blessings.

REGULAR PIONEER SERVICE

Whether you are able to move to another area or not, can you adjust your affairs to spend more time in the urgent work of Kingdom-preaching and disciple-making?

Have you considered the regular pioneer service? Those who participate in this activity devote at least 1,200 hours a year, an average of 100 hours per month, to the field ministry. Because they are able to make themselves available to such an extent for this work, they have the satisfaction of knowing that they can be used by Christ Jesus and the heavenly angels in this enlarged manner in aiding sincere persons to come into association with Jehovah's Christian congregation.

The pioneer service calls for a good personal schedule and diligent work. Three hours and twenty minutes every day, on the average, need to be set aside for the actual field ministry, and the rest of the day remains in which you can care for other responsibilities. You may serve either in your home territory or elsewhere. With careful planning, many thousands of Jehovah's Christian witnesses find that they can do it, and they rejoice to be able to express their love for Jehovah in this way.

Every young person ought to give serious consideration to this field of service. When he completes his years of required secular education, what is he going to do with his life? Does he truly love Jehovah and feel compassion for those people who are unwillingly in bondage to the old system of things? If he is a dedicated, baptized praiser of Jehovah, there should be no doubt. His heart will move him to serve Jehovah whole-souled.

Of course, there are some young folks who find themselves confronted with heavy responsibilities because of unfortunate situations that exist at home; others have severe physical limitations. (1 Tim. 5:4) Though their circumstances limit to some extent what they are able to do in the direct field ministry, they can, nevertheless, be whole-souled in their efforts by making the best use of all the other opportunities that are open to them.

Pioneer service is not limited to any certain age-group. The pioneer ranks include young and old, single and married, the physically strong and some who have limited resources of health. Most of them had obstacles to overcome in order to become pioneers. But deep-seated love for Jehovah, full reliance on him and careful planning have made it possible for tens of thousands to enjoy the pioneer work. Of course, the field ministry is not all that there is to our lives as Christians, and other Scriptural obligations cannot be ignored simply because one prefers the field service. But those who, on examining their own situation, find that they can make the needed adjustments in their lives to become pioneers, and who do so out of love, will enjoy rich blessings at the hand of God.

Do you qualify to enroll as a pioneer? Before applying for pioneer service, the applicant should have been baptized for at least six months, and he should have participated in the field service each month for the past six months. He should also have arranged his personal affairs so that, barring any unforeseen circumstances of a serious nature, he will really be able to devote the required amount of time to the field ministry. Most importantly, he must have a reputation for fine Christian conduct. It should be evident to others that he displays the fruits of God's spirit in both speech and conduct. He should be clean in both body and spirit, free from habits that contaminate the body and impair one's ability to serve Jehovah with one's "whole mind." (Matt. 22:37; 2 Cor. 7:1) He should not be given to extremes in dress and grooming, but his attire and his attitude should reflect favorably upon the congregation that he would represent as an evangelizer.—Compare 1 Timothy 2:9, 10.

If you meet these requirements, you may obtain an application blank from the presiding overseer of your congregation, your circuit overseer or the Watch Tower branch office. Read it carefully and answer all the questions. Then, at least thirty days before you wish to start pioneering, submit the application to your presiding overseer. He, along with the field overseer and the Bible study overseer, will review it. If you meet the qualifications set out in the preceding paragraph, they will recommend that the branch office accept your application. However, if anyone does not qualify, they kindly inform the applicant of the reasons why they cannot recommend him and they do not send the application to the branch office. If you are appointed to be a regular pioneer, notification of appointment will be sent by the Watch Tower Society to the presiding overseer so that an announcement can be made to the congregation, and he will give you the supplies sent for your use.

Though all who are pioneers should be exemplary as Christians, not all have the same abilities. Nor do all serve under the same circumstances. So it is not expected that they will all have the same results. All are encouraged to make good use of the literature provided through the branch office. It is recommended that they determine how many copies of the *Watchtower* and *Awake!* magazines they are able to distribute, and then arrange to receive a regular supply of these. Of course, it is appreciated that their success in distributing literature in connection with the work of Kingdom-preaching will depend to a considerable extent on the response of the people in the territory. Similarly, some pioneers, depending on their ability and the territory where they serve, will have better results in disciple-making than others. But all are urged to appreciate the importance of this latter feature of our work and, with that in mind, to make return calls on those who show interest in the Kingdom message.

Promptly at the end of each month, a pioneer report card is to be filled out and handed to the field overseer of the congregation to which the pioneer is assigned. He notes the figures on the individual's Publisher's Record card in the congregation file. The field overseer also totals the reports for all the regular pioneers in the congregation and enters this combined report on the congregation's monthly report to the branch office. Then he turns the pioneer report cards over to the presiding overseer for signing and mailing to the branch office along with the congregation's report, no later than the sixth of the month.

Those pioneers living in isolated territory send their monthly service report cards directly to the branch office, including on them a notation of any persons that they baptized during the month, if such was the case. So that there will be a record of their service available for consultation during the visit of the circuit overseer, in their case it is advisable to keep for at least a year the slips on which they make daily notation of their field ministry.

If, for some reason, you are unable to report a full 100 hours of field service for certain months, a brief note of explanation should be included on your report card. You should also arrange to make up the time before the service year ends, so that your total report for the entire service year, which runs from September 1 through the following August 31, will be at least 1,200 hours.

As an aid to pioneers in meeting their expenses, they may obtain literature at less than cost. In addition to this, each one must determine for himself how much secular work he needs to do in order to care for his physical needs. The apostle Paul set a fine example by working with his hands so as not to impose an expensive burden on the congregation in whose territory he served. (Acts 18:2-4; 20:33, 34; 2 Thess. 3:7, 8) However, he did not seek luxuries. Pioneers do well to follow that example, "seeking first the kingdom" and looking to God to bless their efforts to obtain the food and covering that they require.—Matt. 6:33.

Pioneers who are assigned to work with a congregation should cooperate closely with the presiding overseer. They should also appreciate the importance of showing active concern for others in the congregation. It is not only our obedience to Christ's command to preach the good news that proves us to be his disciples, but also the 'love that we have among ourselves.' (John 13:34, 35) Nor does our spending much time in preaching to others lessen the need for us to apply in our own lives the high moral standard of God's Word. In regard to Christian conduct, pioneers are required to be exemplary. (2 Cor. 6:3, 4) If any pioneer does not conduct himself in a fine Christian manner despite counsel, it is the responsibility of the body of elders to remove him as a pioneer and notify the branch office of such removal. Such a person will not be enrolled again as a pioneer until the elders in the congregation are convinced that he has completely changed from his former course and until they have seen evidence, over a sufficient period of time, that he truly is determined to conduct himself in a fine Christian manner.

When a pioneer desires a change of assignment because of moving or because he will be in another location for more than three months, he returns his pioneer assignment card through the presiding overseer to the branch office and requests reassignment. The same procedure is followed when a congregation divides and the pioneer finds himself in the territory of a newly formed group. Similarly, pioneers who move to another country, with intention of staying for more than three months, request, through the presiding overseer, that their records be transferred to the branch office under which they will be serving. Then the branch office under which the pioneers are presently serving arranges with the other branch office for assignment of the pioneers in the area where they would like to work.

Anyone who finds it necessary to leave the pioneer ranks may do so by returning his pioneer identification and assignment card, through the presiding overseer, to the branch office. Sometimes circumstances that make this necessary arise in one's life. But, wherever possible, the Society encourages those in the pioneer service to stay on in that ministry, thus continuing to share as fully as possible in publicizing Jehovah's name and kingdom.

TEMPORARY PIONEER SERVICE

There are many of Jehovah's Christian witnesses who, after honestly appraising their personal circumstances, do not find that they can be regular pioneers. But with careful planning and extra effort many thousands are able to pioneer temporarily from time to time, and their whole-souled love for Jehovah moves them to do this. Large numbers of them share in this service during the month of March or April each year, when there is much special activity in the congregations. Others do it during those months when the circuit overseer visits their congregation, or at vacation time or at regular intervals all year long. Every time they serve in this capacity they find it to be an enjoyable and spiritually stimulating experience.

Have you considered being a temporary pioneer? The enrollment requirements are not difficult. To qualify, you must be baptized and have a reputation for good Christian conduct. You should also have made plans that will enable you to devote the required amount of time to the field ministry.

Enrollment for temporary pioneer service is handled right in your own congregation. Ask your presiding overseer for an application, fill it out and then submit it to him sometime before you wish to begin your temporary pioneer service. If possible, give him your application at least a week in advance. The application will not be sent to the branch office, but, rather, will be considered by the presiding overseer, field overseer and the Bible study overseer. If they approve it, announcement of your appointment will be made to the congregation. Then the application will be turned over to those assigned to care for literature and magazine supplies, to notify them of the dates that you will be a temporary pioneer so that they can supply you with literature at pioneer rates for use during that period.

You may enroll as a temporary pioneer for two weeks, or for one, two or more full months. Those who apply agree to devote at least 100 hours to the field service during each full month of their appointment, or, if they will be serving for less than a month, then a minimum of 75 hours for the month.

At the end of the month temporary pioneers turn in their service reports to the congregation in the regular manner, using Field Service Report slips just as all the congregation publishers do. The field overseer enters the figures on their Publisher's Record cards, with a notation that they were temporary pioneers. Then the combined activity of all the temporary pioneers in the congregation is entered in the space provided for that purpose on the congregation's monthly service report that is sent to the branch office.

If you have not yet been a temporary pioneer, we urge you to share in this service. It is within the reach of nearly every baptized proclaimer of the good news at some time during the year. Most of those who do it once are anxious to enroll again.

SPECIAL PIONEER SERVICE

Pioneers who are doing particularly well in aiding others to become disciples and who are free and willing to move to any assignment where they are needed may be invited by the branch office to become special pioneers. Some are assigned to work with congregations that have much territory that is not being regularly covered, but usually they go into isolated territory to carry on the preaching work and establish new congregations.

It has been noted that special pioneers have best results if they select a well-populated portion of their territory and work it thoroughly, covering it again and again. They follow through with repeated calls on persons who show interest and patiently conduct Bible studies with them, at the same time keeping the house-to-house work going on a regular basis. Gradually they try to get those attending the home Bible studies acquainted with one another. In time one of the newly interested persons may be willing to open his home for a study that others are welcome to attend. This provides the basis for a meeting much like the congregation book studies that are sponsored by every congregation. To stimulate the gathering of newly interested ones, public meetings may be planned periodically. Then, as the group manifests readiness to progress, arrangements may be made for the *Watchtower* study and other congregation meetings, one at a time.

Special care needs to be given to acquaint these people with the organization of Jehovah's people and how it operates. The privilege of participating in the Kingdom-preaching work should be kept before them, and, when they qualify, they may be assisted to share in it. This requires patient, steady effort. When men who are associated with the group dedicate themselves to God and get baptized, it is good to give special attention to acquainting them with the various ways that they may in time be able to show their love for Jehovah by accepting responsibility in connection with meetings and arrangements for field service. Then, when the congregation is formed, the special pioneer needs to stay with it to build it up until it is firmly established and able to continue making good progress, with Jehovah's blessing.—Acts 19:1, 8-10; 20:17-21, 31.

Those who accept assignments of service as special pioneers agree to devote 150 hours to the field ministry each month. As they do their work they endeavor to make full use of the fine publications provided by the "faithful and discreet slave" class through the Watch Tower Society. They also give particular attention to the work of disciple-making by calling back on interested persons and conducting home Bible studies. When they baptize any persons, apart from an immersion at an assembly, they note this at the bottom of their monthly field service report to the branch office.

This full program of service leaves little time for secular work; so the Watch Tower Society supplies special pioneers with a nominal money allowance each month that 150 hours of field service are reported, to aid them in obtaining the needed "sustenance and covering." (1 Tim. 6:8) And, as is true of all other pioneers, they receive their literature supplies at less than cost. Additional financial assistance is given to special pioneers about November 1 each year to obtain clothing. These zealous ministers work hard, and at times a change is needed; so provision is made for them to take two weeks off each year, and if they have a record of continuous service in various branches of the pioneer work for twenty years, the vacation time is extended to three weeks.

The branch office is keenly interested in the work of these brothers and keeps in touch with them. In the case of special pioneers in isolated territory, each time around the circuit the circuit overseer spends a full week with them, helping them in any way he can, sharing together in every feature of service, doing personal study with them and having each of the congregation meetings during the course of the week. In this way they are strengthened and encouraged in their ministry. There are special joys in this work of opening up new territory and sharing in the establishment of new congregations. It was a type of service in which the apostle Paul took pleasure, and the record of his ministry can be a source of inspiration to those who make themselves available for special pioneer service.—Rom. 15:20-24.

MISSIONARY SERVICE

The commission that Christ Jesus gave his followers to "make disciples of people of all the nations" and to be his witnesses "to the most distant part of the earth" called for at least some of them to move out into foreign fields, beyond the boundaries of their own homeland. (Matt. 28:19; Acts 1:8) The apostle Peter responded to that need, traveling east as far as Babylon; and Paul and his associates made known the good news throughout Asia Minor and Greece. They had a real missionary spirit. Could you make yourself available for service of that sort?

There is still a need for missionaries who are able to go into other lands in our day, and it is gratifying to know that young men and women are taking up this work. Those who enter such missionary service and stay there are not persons who indifferently reason that, after all, God could use someone else to do the job. To the contrary, their heartfelt love for Jehovah moves them to volunteer in the spirit of that faithful prophet Isaiah, who said: "Here I am! Send me." (Isa. 6:8) They know that the Kingdom good news is to be preached "in all the inhabited earth," and they are pleased to be used by God in this way. (Matt. 24:14) Their faith gives them the conviction that, no matter where they are on earth, Jehovah will look after them as long as they are busy doing his will.

Those who are sent into foreign missionary service are, in most instances, first given special training at the Watchtower Bible School of Gilead in Brooklyn, New York. Here they make an intensive study of the Bible, receive instruction in organizational matters and usually are helped to acquire a foundation knowledge of another language.

The prospective missionaries who are invited to attend Gilead School are selected from among persons who meet the following qualifications: baptized at least three years; full-time service for the past two years; generally, between the ages of 21 and 40; single, or married at least two years and with no dependent children. They must know the English language. Those who apply should have good health; they should be willing to serve anywhere; and they should plan to stay in their missionary assignment, making it their home. Applications may be requested from the Watch Tower Society or they may be obtained and filled out at special meetings arranged for this purpose at most district assemblies.

Missionaries carry on their work in the same way as do the special pioneers, devoting a minimum of 150 hours a month to the field ministry. However, where possible, the Watch Tower Society provides a missionary home from which a group of them can carry on their work and sees to it that they are able to obtain the needed food. In addition, each missionary is given some financial assistance once a year to obtain clothing, as well as a small monthly allowance for personal items, if he is meeting the monthly requirement of 150 hours in the field ministry. There is also a vacation provision each year, as for special pioneers.

At first the customs and foods in another country may seem strange, but soon one grows accustomed to them. A loving desire to aid the people to learn the truth about God and his kingdom makes any inconveniences in a changed way of life pale out of sight. As the missionary sees the truth of God's Word bring about changes in the lives of those whom he teaches, he cannot but be humbly thankful that Jehovah has privileged him to share in this work. What a thrill it has been to the missionaries to see congregations grow up in the territory where they serve, and to know that persons with whom they studied have become loyal servants of God! Jehovah has indeed blessed them because they have worked hard in his service and have done so with a willing heart.

BETHEL SERVICE

Ordained ministers who serve at Bethel must be whole-souled in their love for Jehovah, his Word and the Christian congregation, and should be motivated by a strong desire to serve on behalf of their Christian brothers. It is necessary for the Watch Tower Society to operate Bethel homes, branch offices and printing plants in order to supply Jehovah's witnesses around the globe with Bibles and Bible literature for their personal study, for use in congregation meetings and for distribution in the field ministry. All the work done in this connection is very much appreciated by Jehovah's Christian witnesses throughout the earth.

There is work of many kinds done at Bethel. Some have office assignments; others do typesetting, run printing presses, bind books or prepare literature for mailing. In addition, it is necessary to have workers who care for the home, wash clothes and cook and serve meals. All of this is done to further the Kingdom interests.

Bethel family members start their day's activity early. Gathered at the breakfast table, they enjoy a thorough discussion of the day's Scripture text and comments. After breakfast they go to their assigned work, at which they spend at least 8 hours and 40 minutes a day for five days of the week, and four hours on Saturdays. Monday evenings the members of the family study the *Watchtower* lesson for the week and attend the family's Theocratic Ministry School. Other evenings as well as Saturday afternoon and Sunday are used for attending congregation meetings, sharing in the field ministry and attending to personal matters. Those who have been appointed as elders at Bethel also have the privilege of giving public talks in nearby congregations. The schedule is a full one and richly rewarding in a spiritual way.

Applicants for Bethel service must have been baptized for at least a year, and preference is shown for those who are pioneers. The work to be done requires good health, ability to do hard work and willingness to do whatever is assigned. Most of the ones invited to live and work at Bethel are single brothers, between seventeen and thirty-five years of age; though at times sisters are invited, and some married couples without dependent children. The ones whose applications are accepted agree to serve at Bethel for at least four years, but any who can do so are encouraged to stay beyond that and make service at Bethel their life's work. If you meet these qualifications and want to serve at Bethel, you may obtain an application from your circuit overseer, from the branch office or at one of the meetings arranged for Bethel applicants at most district assemblies.

Members of the Bethel family are well cared for. They are provided with a comfortable room and good food. There is a small monthly allowance to cover personal expenses, and each year financial assistance is provided to help them to obtain needed clothing. Time is also allowed for a two-week vacation, and three weeks for those who have served for twenty years. The physical provisions to sustain them are made possible through the contributions of Jehovah's Christian witnesses world wide to the branch offices, and the Bethel family appreciates these things.

Bethel is a marvelous place to serve. In such a theocratic atmosphere as exists at Bethel homes there is excellent opportunity for spiritual growth. It is richly rewarding to work all day in association with others who love Jehovah and to know that one's work benefits so many of Jehovah's people.

WHAT YOU PERSONALLY ARE ABLE TO DO

Of course, not everyone is in position to serve at Bethel or to devote many hours in the field ministry as a pioneer or a missionary. But all of us can and should be whole-souled in our ministry. When we consider what God has done for us through Christ Jesus, it should move us deeply. As the apostle Paul wrote to the Corinthians: "For the love the Christ has compels us, because this is what we have judged, that one man died for all; so, then, all had died; and he died for all that those who live might live no longer for themselves, but for him who died for them and was raised up." —2 Cor. 5:14, 15.

Is that true of you? Are you living no longer for yourself? Is your entire life truly built around your relationship to Jehovah through Christ Jesus? Are there ways in which you could share more fully in the work that they are having done in the earth today?

No matter where we serve or in what capacity, we cannot afford to let ourselves become complacent, reasoning that we are having some share in Jehovah's service and, after all, that is the important thing. "Do not loiter" in serving Jehovah, but "be aglow with the spirit," is the apostolic counsel. It is good for each one of us seriously to consider the question: Is love for Jehovah, his Son Christ Jesus and my fellowman impelling me to render whole-souled service to Jehovah? —Rom. 12:11.

CHAPTER 8

FINANCING THE WORK OF PREACHING AND DISCIPLE-MAKING

A QUESTION frequently asked by persons who are newly associated with Jehovah's witnesses is, Who provides the money for carrying on this work? The answer is that Jehovah's Christian witnesses everywhere have a part in it.

Jehovah's witnesses are aware of the fact that much work is being done under the direction of the Watch Tower Society to further the preaching of the good news, they know that it requires money, and they want to have a share in providing it. They are free to send voluntary contributions to the nearest branch office of the Watch Tower Bible and Tract Society. They have proved to be like God's servants in ancient times who brought, 'everyone whose heart impelled him, a voluntary offering to Jehovah.' (Ex. 35:20-29) Most of the donations received are in relatively small amounts, but these, when added together, provide enough to keep the work going. (Luke 21:1-4) Some gifts are received from estates, under wills of Jehovah's witnesses.

It is a privilege to share in this way in furthering the work in all parts of the earth, and none need feel that what they are able to offer is too little to be worth while. As 2 Corinthians 8:12 says: "If the readiness is there first, it is especially acceptable according to what a person has, not according to what a person does not have." Contributions are received through the branch offices from individuals, congregations and circuits. These donations are appreciatively acknowledged.

Some of the money contributed is used to build and maintain printing plants where Bible literature is produced; and the ordained ministers who care for this assignment are supplied with "sustenance and covering" and a small allowance for personal expenses. (1 Tim. 6:8; 5:18) Others who are devoting their time and energy in serving as missionaries in foreign lands, special pioneers, and circuit and district overseers are also given assistance so that they will have the food and shelter required as they carry on their work. Additionally, literature is provided at less than cost to them as well as to regular pioneers and temporary pioneers to help to defray their expenses. At times help is given in providing necessities for faithful brothers and sisters who have been the victims of disasters such as floods or earthquakes so that they will be able to continue in their ministry. All of this is made possible by voluntary contributions sent to the branch offices.—Rom. 15:26; 1 Cor. 16:1-4.

EXPENSES WITHIN EACH CONGREGATION

Within each congregation there are also expenses that must be met. No collection is ever taken, nor is there any assessment of dues, but contribution boxes are provided at our meeting places so that each one can have a part, "just as he has resolved in his heart." —2 Cor. 9:7.

This money is used principally to provide a Kingdom Hall in which the congregation can meet, and to care for its upkeep. If there is more money than is needed to care for these expenses, the body of elders may discuss how those funds can best be used to further the work of preaching and disciple-making. Then they present to the congregation a written resolution containing their recommendations. Sometimes as an expression of loving assistance, a congregation may give financial help to a nearby congregation, perhaps one that is dividing off from it, in order to enable it to build its own Kingdom Hall. In some cases, the congregation may request that a portion of the money be sent to the branch office for use in furthering the Kingdom work in other areas.

What is done if a situation should arise in which brothers or sisters in a congregation are in need of material assistance due to advanced age, infirmity or other adversity? In many places the state makes provision for needy persons, if they make application for it. Also, each one in the congregation has the privilege of demonstrating on a personal basis his loving concern. As the apostle John wrote: "Whoever has this world's means for supporting life and beholds his brother having need and yet shuts the door of his tender compassions upon him, in what way does the love of God remain in him? Little children, let us love, neither in word nor with the tongue, but in deed and truth." —1 John 3:17, 18; compare 2 Thessalonians 3:6-12.

At times the local body of elders may even consider what can be done by the congregation as a whole in the case of certain needy brothers and sisters who have a long record of faithful service in advancing the interests of pure worship. (Compare 1 Timothy 5:9, 10.) However, as in the first-century congregation, if there are children and grandchildren, then it is their obligation, not that of the congregation, to care for aged parents and grandparents that are in need. This is in agreement with Paul's counsel to an overseer in Ephesus: "Honor widows that are actually widows. But if any widow has children or grandchildren, let these learn first to practice godly devotion in their own household and to keep paying a due compensation to their parents and grandparents, for this is acceptable in God's sight."—1 Tim. 5:3, 4; compare Matthew 15:3-9.

None of the overseers receive a salary for the work that they do in the congregation. It is true that the work they do on behalf of their brothers may require many hours, and some of them may even cut down on the amount of secular work that they do, in order to have more time for the congregation. But they do this out of love for Jehovah and for his "sheep," not with expectation of any material gain. If those with whom they serve become aware that certain ones could benefit from some assistance in order to continue in their ministry, they may, out of appreciation for the labors of love on their behalf, want to do something to help. This would be a voluntary expression on their part.—1 Tim. 5:17, 18.

Apart from any monetary contributions that Jehovah's witnesses may make to the congregation and any material help that they may give to deserving ones in their midst, all of them personally contribute time and effort to the preaching of the good news in their territory. They are willing to bear their own expenses in this, and they expect no money in return for the assistance that they offer to those with whom they study the Bible. They apply the instructions of Christ Jesus, who said: "You received free, give free."—Matt. 10:8.

ORDERLY HANDLING OF
LITERATURE AND FUNDS

Each congregation receives and distributes magazines and other literature as a means of spreading the good news. This involves the handling of money, but it does not enrich individuals or the congregation.

Usually, one of the ministerial servants is assigned by the body of elders to care for the congregation's supply of magazines. Those who want magazines, either for personal study or for distribution, are requested to place an order with him to receive a given number of each issue. An order for the total number required is submitted to the branch office on the magazine Distributors' Order blank. It is very much appreciated when each one who orders magazines takes them. The congregation obtains them from the branch office on credit, and it depends on each one to take his supply so that the account does not become delinquent.

When the magazines are received from the branch office, the brother who cares for them informs the one who cares for congregation accounts of the issue and the number of magazines received, and this is compared with the total shown on the label on the package. (If there is any discrepancy, the presiding overseer should be asked to notify the branch office.) The magazines are then made available to the congregation. Each person is requested to pay for the magazines when he receives them.

The body of elders also assigns someone, generally a ministerial servant, to care for the supplies of books, booklets, Bibles and tracts received by the congregation. Using his records from years past as a guide, he can estimate how much of certain items to order, so that there will be sufficient but not an excess. In most congregations an order is sent to the branch office just once a month, at the beginning of the month. Usually most of the literature in stock is obtained on credit. When a shipment of literature is received from the branch office, the one caring for literature supplies checks it against the invoice or packing list to be sure that everything is in order. The invoice or list is then turned over to the person who cares for the accounts. Any discrepancies are to be reported to the branch office by the presiding overseer.

The one caring for the supplies has a responsibility to take good care of them, keeping them neat and clean, and to keep accurate records. Whenever literature is obtained from him, he is to make note of the amount taken. A progressive inventory kept by the congregation tells what is on hand at any time. Additionally, each year, on September 1, it is requested that an actual-count inventory be made and a report sent to the branch office.

Another qualified person, preferably a ministerial servant other than the ones who care for the magazines and other literature supplies, is charged by the body of elders with the responsibility of caring for money that is contributed for the advancement of the Kingdom work, as well as funds handled by the congregation in connection with magazines, other literature, subscriptions, and so forth. He is to keep a careful record of all money received and disbursed. The method of accounting used is outlined in detail in instructions provided to each congregation by the branch office.

After each meeting any money in the contribution box is removed. At least once a week money is also received from the brothers who care for magazines and other literature. Receipts are made out in duplicate for all such money received, and appropriate entries are made on the Account Sheet. The money for magazines and other literature is to be remitted to the branch office once a month, by the sixth of the month.

When someone obtains a subscription, or wants to renew his own, it is requested that the slip be made out neatly and accurately and submitted *in duplicate*. These may be given to the brother who cares for accounts and he will see that they get prompt attention. For the total money received at any one meeting he makes out a Receipt for the congregation's records. Once a week he gives the originals of the subscription slips to the presiding overseer, with covering Remittance and Credit Request form and corresponding remittance, to be checked and sent to the branch office. He keeps the duplicate subscription slips, each marked "Copy," in the congregation files, with a note for each group as to when they were mailed, in case any questions are raised by subscribers.

Since the money handled belongs to the congregation,

or involves its accounts with the branch office, each month the one handling the accounts prepares a financial report to be read to the congregation. Also, the presiding overseer arranges to have the accounts audited every three months.

Some congregations find it convenient to have a bank account in which to deposit their funds each week. The account is in the name of the " . . . . . Congregation of Jehovah's Witnesses." If there is more than one congregation in the city, then the other congregation of Jehovah's witnesses should have its own name. All checks drawn on the account are signed by two persons designated by the body of elders, which persons may be signers for any number of years. Other congregations may prefer to use money orders, bank drafts or some other safe means of transmitting money. In every case, however, the expenditures are approved by the presiding overseer.

EXPENSES FOR
OPERATING CIRCUIT ASSEMBLIES

As is true in individual congregations, so, too, at circuit assemblies contribution boxes are provided and the expenses are cared for by contributions from the brothers in the circuit. A brother assigned by the circuit overseer cares for this money and pays bills that have been approved by the circuit overseer. (This brother who cares for circuit accounts is not assigned for any specified period of time.) If there is not enough money on hand to care for the initial expenses, the circuit overseer may advise the congregations in the circuit of their privilege to assist with expenses. But usually after the first assembly in any circuit there are sufficient funds on hand to care for the initial expenses of the next assembly. Between assemblies this money is often deposited with the branch office. However, if there is a deficit at the conclusion of the assembly, it is the responsibility of the elders in the congregations to discuss among themselves what contributions their congregations are in position to make to the circuit funds to care for the expenses, and then to handle this with their respective congregations by means of a resolution.

When any purchases of equipment for the circuit are made, when donations are sent to the branch office, or when there are other expenditures out of the ordinary, these matters involving the use of *available* circuit funds are decided by the congregation elders at their meeting on Sunday morning at the assembly. Authorization of such expenditures is always put in writing in the form of a resolution, which is voted on by these elders, and such matters that will be of particular interest and encouragement to the brothers may thereafter be announced.

This care given to the handling of funds of the congregations assures that the money will all be used in the way intended, to advance the Kingdom interests.

CHAPTER 9

SAFEGUARDING THE CLEANNESS OF THE CONGREGATION

JEHOVAH'S Christian witnesses are a clean people. They must be so to have God's favor and blessing. Preaching God's Word to others is not enough; we must live in harmony with it. To his anointed brothers in the early Christian congregation, Peter wrote: "As obedient children, quit being fashioned according to the desires you formerly had in your ignorance, but, in accord with the Holy One who called you, do you also become holy yourselves in all your conduct, because it is written: 'You must be holy, because I am holy.'" —1 Pet. 1:14-16.

In the Bible the word "holy" conveys the idea of that which is fresh, untarnished or clean, whether in a physical or a spiritual or moral sense. (2 Cor. 7:1) How do we "become holy"? Through the sanctifying power of the truth that sets us apart from the world of mankind alienated from God and apart from its practices of unrighteousness. (John 17:16-19; Num. 15:40; 2 Cor. 6:14-18) We must be obedient to the truth with genuine, heartfelt love for God and his righteousness and for our brothers if we are to remain clean in this way. (1 Thess. 3:12, 13; 1 Pet. 1:22) Only then will God's spirit, which is also holy, guide us. At times God may discipline us, and, while unpleasant in itself, this discipline is done in love, "for our profit that we may partake of his holiness." (Heb. 12:5-11) He wants us to gain life everlasting, not to suffer destruction.

While on earth, Christ Jesus set the example for those who would form his congregation of anointed followers. His purpose is finally to "present the congregation to himself in its splendor . . . holy and without blemish." (Eph. 5:25-27) He laid the groundwork for this, not only by his own righteous example and by the purifying message he brought, but also by his ransom sacrifice by means of which sins may be forgiven.

After Jesus' death and resurrection, the apostles and others taking the lead among the early Christians showed great concern for maintaining the purity of the congregation. (Acts 20:26-32; 2 Cor. 11:2, 3; 2 Pet. 1:9-11; 3:14; Jude 3, 4) Today the same concern is shown. Not only the anointed remnant, but the great crowd of "other sheep" appreciate the need for keeping their identification (represented by white robes) as clean servants of God, separate from the world. —Rev. 3:4; 7:9, 14; 19:8.

PERSONAL DIFFICULTIES AND FRICTIONS

Wherever dissension and disunity exist, there is evidence of some unclean force working. James said that jealousy and contention are from an "earthly, animal, demonic" source and produce "disorder and every vile thing," working against what is chaste. (Jas. 3:14-18; compare 4:1-8.) All of us are, of course, imperfect in ourselves, sinners by inheritance. (1 John 1:8) We all make mistakes; we say or do things we thereafter regret. While we can and should improve as time goes along, during this system of things we will never be completely free from our errors. (Rom. 7:14-25; Jas. 3:2) Recognizing this, God counsels us through his Word that we should have "intense love for one another, because love covers a multitude of sins." (1 Pet. 4:8) The inspired apostle John frankly states that "he who does not love his brother, whom he has seen, cannot be loving God, whom he has not seen."—1 John 4:20.

This calls for much mercy and forgiveness on our part. The Scriptures admonish: "Continue putting up with one another and forgiving one another freely if anyone has a cause for complaint against another.

Even as Jehovah freely forgave you, so do you also." (Col. 3:13) Only those who are forgiving and compassionate in their dealings with others can expect forgiveness and mercy from God.—Matt. 5:7; 6:12, 14, 15.

So, when difficulties arise between members of the congregation, mature Christians do not vengefully seek to cause injury to the one they feel has injured them. (1 Pet. 3:8, 9) Nor do they treat him coldly, refusing to talk to him anymore. (1 Cor. 13:4, 5; Eph. 4:26) They prefer to overlook offenses, especially so when they realize that they have not been committed with malice. (Eph. 4:31, 32) As Proverbs 19:11 states: "The insight of a man certainly slows down his anger, and it is beauty on his part to pass over transgression." —Compare Ecclesiastes 7:8, 9.

'IF YOUR BROTHER
COMMITS A SIN AGAINST YOU'

This willingness to overlook offenses and to forgive does not mean that we are not concerned about wrongdoing or that we approve it. Not all wrongs can simply be charged to inherited imperfection; nor is it for our brother's good or for the good of the congregation to overlook it if he commits wrongs that go beyond minor offenses. (Lev. 19:17; Ps. 141:5; Luke 17:3) Under the Law covenant given through Moses there was recognition of a difference in degrees of seriousness of sins and transgressions. This is also true for Christians under the new covenant.—Compare 1 John 5:16, 17.

Jesus gave counsel concerning sins that might be committed against a person and be considered as too serious in nature to be overlooked. He said: "If your brother commits a sin, go lay bare his fault between you and him alone. If he listens to you, you have gained your brother. But if he does not listen, take along with you one or two more, in order that at the mouth of two or three witnesses every matter may be established. If he does not listen to them, speak to the congregation. If he does not listen even to the congregation, let him be to you just as a man of the nations and as a tax collector." (Matt. 18:15-17) Jesus' listeners, being Jewish, knew that for others of his people to look upon a Jew as a "man of the nations and as a tax collector" would mean his being viewed as cast out of the Jewish congregation.

Since the steps that Jesus set forth could lead to such a serious consequence, he was obviously not setting out a formula for the handling of every petty offense against an individual. Of course, many times it is the proper and wise and very helpful thing to go and talk to someone where personal difficulty exists because of some minor offense, doing this with the aim of healing any breach that seems to be developing. (Matt. 6:14, 15; Prov. 12:18) Many misunderstandings are cleared up in this way. But evidently this was not what Jesus was speaking of at this time. He referred, not to mere personal differences, but to offenses serious enough to merit one's expulsion from the congregation.

Before ever you would initiate the procedure set out at Matthew 18:15-17, then, you should have definite proof that such a serious sin was indeed committed against you. Jesus did not say, 'If you *think* your brother has sinned.' You should consider the counsel at Proverbs 25:8-10 so that you do not start something that will only bring shame and humiliation upon yourself. Even where the proof exists, you should not spread the matter abroad, gossiping about it, but should go to the offender privately and "lay bare his fault between you and him alone."

If your brother "listens," accepting your reproof, then "you have gained your brother." Does this refer simply to effecting a personal reconciliation? No, but as the rest of Jesus' counsel shows, it must mean 'gaining him' in the sense of helping him to stay within the congregation, turning him back from a course that could lead to his being expelled therefrom, with accompanying loss of God's favor and blessing. So, the 'gaining' of your brother would be in the sense described at James 5:19, 20, Galatians 6:1 and Jude 22, 23. This, in fact, should be your principal aim and desire—not that of getting personal relief or satisfaction for some offense.

Where the sinner accepts reproof and seeks forgiveness, Jesus states, there is no need to carry the matter farther. This fact shows that, although serious, the offenses here discussed were limited in nature to such as could be settled between the individuals involved. This would not include such offenses as fornication, adultery, homosexuality, blasphemy, apostasy, idolatry and similar grave sins, for under the Law covenant then in force, these sins required more than forgiveness from an offended individual.—1 Cor. 6:9, 10; Gal. 5:19-21.

In view of this, and in view of the illustration that Jesus subsequently gave, as recorded at Matthew 18: 21-35, the sins here considered evidently were sins such as those involving financial or property matters—failing to make proper payment for something, some action involving a measure of fraud—or perhaps damaging one's reputation by actual slander, or similar sins. In these cases, if the offender recognized his wrong, expressed willingness to right it to the extent possible, and sought forgiveness, the matter could be settled by the offended one's granting forgiveness.—Compare Matthew 5:25, 26; Luke 12:58.

But what if you take this initial step and the one sinning does not respond? Due to the seriousness of the offense, you cannot simply dismiss the matter. Jesus' counsel shows that you should seek out one or two others and return to talk to the offender. Reasonably these should be witnesses to the wrong. They do not go as mere neutral observers or mediators trying to effect a reconciliation or compromise solution. Instead, you take them with you so that, because of having witnessed the wrong, they can add their testimony to yours. They can also serve as hearers of what is then said. If the matter takes a further step and comes before "the congregation" and the offender denies or alters certain statements or admissions made, these others can give their testimony and bring out the facts. Hopefully this further step will not be necessary and the individual will respond to the combined efforts made to restore him to a course of righteousness. If so, then the matter is closed.

If the offender still refuses to admit his guilt, then what? The matter should now be brought to the attention of the responsible members of the congregation, those of the body of elders assigned to serve in a judicial capacity. It is hoped that the individual will now listen to their official judgment and be "gained" as a person fit to remain in the congregation. If not, then he is disfellowshiped, thereafter to be treated as an outsider.—Matt. 18:17.

THE JUDICIAL COMMITTEE

Today, in each congregation where there are sufficient elders, three of these are assigned to serve as a judicial committee. Usually these will be the ones who, during that year, are serving as presiding overseer, field overseer and Bible study overseer. In the absence of one of these, the others serving as judges may select another elder to serve in his place.

It may be that one of the three customary members of the judicial committee will want to step aside because of his needing to serve as a witness in the matter being considered, or being otherwise involved therein.

Where there are not sufficient elders to form such a committee of three, nearby congregations can be called on to supply those needed, if some matter requiring judicial attention arises.

These representative elders would come together in Jesus' name; seeking Jehovah's guidance in prayer through Christ Jesus, they would not be acting in an independent or arbitrary manner. They would be recognizing Jehovah's headship and the headship of his Son over the entire Christian congregation. Doing this, they would be obligated to recognize as well the vital need to maintain unity with all others under that headship.—1 Cor. 1:10.

They should not be hesitant or fearful of shouldering the responsibility assigned them in such matters, nor of reaching decisions. (1 Cor. 6:1-6) By faithfulness and humble submission to Jehovah and his Son and by sincere prayer for their guidance by holy spirit, they should be able to reach the right conclusion on the matter. The apostle Paul showed confidence in God's direction of the judgment of the elders in Corinth. —2 Cor. 2:10. Compare Matthew 18:19, 20.

HELPING REPENTANT ONES
OVERTAKEN IN TRESPASSES

As fellow members in the 'association of brothers' we should care for one another and strive to protect and strengthen one another. (1 Pet. 5:9) When any of our brothers show weakness we should mercifully go to their aid. The inspired writers of the early Christian congregation make clear that God is pleased when we manifest such sincere interest and concern.

Jude wrote that we should "continue showing mercy to some that have doubts; save them by snatching them out of the fire. But continue showing mercy to others, doing so with fear, while you hate even the inner garment that has been stained by the flesh." (Jude 21-23) So, we do not approve of wrongdoing; we hate it and we stand firm for God's righteous standards, always upholding them. But we do not stop showing mercy to persons when they come into danger due to wrong thinking or weakness; we mercifully take action to restore them.

At James 5:19, 20 the further counsel is given: "My brothers, if anyone among you is misled from the truth and another turns him back, know that he who turns a sinner back from the error of his way will save his soul from death and will cover a multitude of sins." Not only when the sin was personally against us, but in all cases we seek to 'gain our brother,' endeavoring to turn him back from a course that could lead to divine rejection and the condemnation of death.

The elders in the congregation are particularly concerned with doing this as shepherds of the flock. To them, Paul's exhortation at Galatians 6:1 is especially fitting: "Brothers, even though a man takes some false step before he is aware of it, you who have spiritual qualifications try to readjust such a man in a spirit of mildness, as you each keep an eye on yourself, for fear you also may be tempted."

To apply this counsel, we must keep in mind that it is one thing willfully to plan, scheme and work toward some wrong act, craving it (2 Pet. 2:10-22; Jude 4, 8, 10, 12), and another thing to be 'overtaken' in such, stumbling into sin, being 'ensnared' by the Devil. (2 Tim. 2:25, 26) Then, too, there is a difference between a single act of sin and the practice of sin.—1 John 2:1; 3:4-6, 8.

The Scriptures admonish us to "flee" from all forms of wrongdoing—fornication, idolatry, love of money, and so forth. (1 Cor. 6:18; 10:14; 1 Tim. 6:9-11) Some do not deliberately seek such practices, nor try to corrupt the congregation, but they may drift into a spiritually weak condition where they are easily "overreached" by the subtle influence of some sinful temptation. (2 Cor. 2:11) Or, one may even have been following a generally good and upright course but, suddenly, under strong pressure that caught him by surprise, he was not successful in 'fleeing' the wrongdoing and was 'overtaken' by it. He may have committed some immoral or idolatrous act, or a violation of his integrity as regards separateness from the world, perhaps due to not having prepared his heart sufficiently to resist pressure. Yet his conscience may have struck him immediately and, like Peter after denying Christ, he may have gone away and "wept bitterly," being genuinely repentant, cut to the heart.—Luke 22:61, 62.

This is quite different from, for example, the case of Ananias and Sapphira. For a single offense they were put to death by God. But they had conspired to try to deceive the apostles and put on a false front; they were not 'taking some false step before they were aware of it,' nor being "overreached" due to weakness, but planned and worked the sin out themselves. And, of course, in their case God read their hearts and enabled Peter miraculously to see through their subterfuge. —Acts 5:1-11.

The elders, as overseers and shepherds, are concerned about any of God's flock who may stray. They do not act as 'spiritual policemen' in arresting wrongdoing, nor do they serve as mere judges enforcing justice and imposing sentence on violators of what is right. While having deep respect for God's righteousness and his holiness, at the same time they are concerned with imitating God in manifesting merciful compassion. (Matt. 23:23) Not wanting to lose any of the "sheep" committed to their care, and knowing they will have to "render an account," these shepherds should follow the example of Jehovah God and Christ Jesus in lovingly 'watching over' or overseeing the flock. (Heb. 13: 17; John 17:11, 12, 14; Acts 20:28-30; 1 Pet. 5:2-4) So they are mercifully to seek to rescue any erring ones, restoring them to God's favor.

SEEKING THE HELP OF SHEPHERDS

In view of this, when a baptized member of the congregation commits a serious sin, what should he do?

He should first pray for God's forgiveness through Christ Jesus, confessing his wrong and determining to correct his wrong course. (Ps. 32:5; Prov. 28:13; 1 Tim. 2:5; Matt. 6:12) Then he should not hesitate in approaching any of the spiritually qualified elders of the congregation, seeking their help. As James 5:14-16 says: "Is there anyone sick [spiritually so, as the later reference to sins indicates] among you? Let him call the older men of the congregation to him, and let them pray over him, greasing him with oil in the name of Jehovah. And the prayer of faith will make the indisposed one well, and Jehovah will raise him up. Also, if he has committed sins, it will be forgiven him. Therefore openly confess your sins to one another and pray for one another, that you may get healed. A righteous man's supplication, when it is at work, has much force."

The assistance that these "shepherds" can render is Jehovah's provision made for our good. It is not that we must go through them as intermediaries to gain God's forgiveness. We get that by our confessing to God our wrong, by our repentance and our 'turning around,' leaving the wrong course and making straight paths for our feet. Christ Jesus is our heavenly Helper and High Priest in God's presence.—1 John 1:9; 2:1, 2; Heb. 4:14-16; 7:25.

True, the elders can add their prayers of intercession on our behalf, and these prayers have value with God. The one who has sinned may feel condemned in his heart. In that case the intercessory prayer of the elders would be especially beneficial. (Jas. 5:14-16; 1 Tim. 2:1; 1 John 5:16) So, a person's going to them is to get help. His confessing his wrongdoing to them is for that purpose, as James shows. Obviously, when a person commits grievous sin it is evidence of spiritual weakness or sickness. A person in this position needs help to overcome his difficulties and to regain spiritual health and strength, and he is wise if he humbly asks for that help.

There is grave danger in not asking for assistance. If a brother in difficulty fails to do this, he may easily repeat his sin and even become habituated in it. Or, because of feeling ashamed of his wrong, he may feel uncomfortable among his brothers, not able to enjoy fully his fellowship with them. Or because of a weakened spiritual condition, he may suffer an even greater loss—that of a confident relationship with his heavenly Father. He may feel that there is a 'cloud mass blocking his approach to God, that his prayer may not pass through.' (Lam. 3:44) To isolate himself from the congregation would only compound the danger. (Prov. 18:1) How much better, then, to acknowledge humbly his need for help and avail himself of Jehovah's kind provisions through his Son and through those serving under his Son's headship.

COUNSELING THOSE COMMITTING MINOR TRESPASSES

When a member of the congregation approaches an elder due to having committed some wrong and now seeking help, what should the elder do? Perhaps there was a degree of loose conduct or immoderation in private use of alcoholic beverages; or the person, in his secular relations with those outside the congregation, may have engaged in some form of dishonesty which, though the "accepted" practice among worldlings, he recognizes as being out of harmony with Bible principles. If the fault was not of a grave nature, not a gross sin nor one bringing public reproach, and the person openly acknowledges the wrong and manifests sincere repentance, it may suffice for the elder whom he approaches to give him some good counsel and admonition.

In such cases, however, it would be good for the elder approached to inform the one serving as presiding overseer, telling him about the matter and what counsel he gave. The one serving as presiding overseer may have had more experience in such matters than the elder initially approached. He may have some helpful suggestions to add, or may have knowledge of the matter that makes advisable some further admonishing of the person or discussion with him.

In other cases, however, the sin committed may have brought the congregation into public disrepute. It may be one that puts the congregation into a bad position before Jehovah, reproaching his name. The offense may have been loose conduct of a gross nature, bordering on fornication; or actual fornication, adultery or other

serious sexual immorality may be involved. The sin may
not be just one instance of drunkenness, lying or stealing
but repeated cases of such wrong acts. It may be such
as would readily become a matter of discussion in the
congregation. In all such cases the matter should be
brought to the attention of those elders serving in a
judicial capacity in the congregation.

HEARINGS BEFORE THE JUDICIAL COMMITTEE

Where such matters come to the attention of the
judicial committee they should arrange to meet with
those involved. In some cases it will not be a matter
in which an individual voluntarily seeks aid. Rather,
an accusation may be brought against some member
of the congregation. The committee should consider
whether the accusation gives some evidence of having
substance or not. If it does, then they should invite the
accused person or persons to meet with them. To avoid
any misunderstanding as to time and place and the
purpose of the meeting, it would be best to put the
invitation in writing, informing the person as to what
his course of action is supposed to have been. He should
be treated in a kind manner. The elders would certainly want the one accused to have the opportunity to
bring along any persons he desires as witnesses on his
behalf and they should make this known to him. If
he does not come to the meeting, they should endeavor
to find a time that is agreeable to him and arrange to
have the meeting then. If someone repeatedly fails
or refuses to come to such a hearing, then the committee must arrive at a decision on the basis of the evidence and testimony available, providing this is sufficient to establish the facts clearly.—Compare Numbers
16:12-14, 25-33.

Judgment of matters affecting the lives of servants
of Jehovah carries with it a great responsibility, and,
for that reason, the judicial committee is obligated to
be sure that it has all the facts before it renders its
decision. (1 Tim. 5:21; Prov. 18:13; Deut. 13:12-14) For
a matter to be established as true, there must be two
or three witnesses. (1 Tim. 5:19; Deut. 19:15; Heb.
10:28) These cannot be persons who are simply repeat-
ing what they have heard from someone else; they
must be witnesses themselves of things concerning

which they testify. No action is taken if there is just one witness; it is not that the brothers discredit the testimony, but the Bible requires that, unless the wrongdoer himself admits his sin, the facts must be substantiated by two or three witnesses in these serious matters.

A person may come and confess a serious wrongdoing and implicate another with him. If the other person denies any sharing in the wrong, then the charge cannot be accepted without additional testimony to provide the necessary two or three witnesses; the committee would not act against the one accused. But the person confessing would be counseled and reproved as necessary, for he has either committed the deed he confesses or is guilty of lying, or both. If he is repentant, he would not be disfellowshiped for the wrong he confesses. But if he later is found to have lied against his brother, there would likely be need to take action against the false accuser. His having lied would place in serious question the genuineness of the "repentant" attitude he may have displayed earlier. Those bearing false witness in Israel were to receive the same treatment they sought to bring upon the one they falsely accused.—Deut. 19:17-21.

On the other hand, if the one accused (but who denies the charge) is actually guilty, we may be sure that Jehovah knows, and in time the truth will become known to his people. (1 Tim. 5:24) Holding to the Scriptural rule of two or three witnesses, however, the elders will be guilty of no injustice.

REPROVING AND RESTORING REPENTANT WRONGDOERS

Even as there are comparative degrees of gravity of wrongdoing so there are comparative degrees of reproof or other action to be applied to the wrongdoers. This calls for wisdom and discernment on the part of those serving in a judicial capacity. They must weigh matters carefully, thinking in terms of principles rather than of rigid rules. Each case should be judged on its own circumstances and merits.

Concerning certain wrongdoers in Crete, Paul wrote Titus to "keep on reproving them *with severity*, that they may be healthy in the faith." (Titus 1:10-13) Of others who were 'caught in the snare of the Devil,' he wrote Timothy to instruct them *"with mildness,"* and he used a similar expression to the Galatians regarding the man who "takes some false step before he is aware of it." (2 Tim. 2:24-26; Gal. 6:1) What will guide a judicial committee in determining what kind of reproof to give a repentant wrongdoer and how best to aid him to be spiritually restored? How also can they protect "the way of the truth" from being "spoken of abusively"?—2 Pet. 2:2.

When a case of wrongdoing is grave enough to require a hearing, the facts should be determined establishing guilt or innocence, but the committee should also seek to ascertain other factors as well. If a serious offense was committed, what were the circumstances leading up to it? Was there evidence of the person's craving wrongful things or 'courting trouble'? Had he been admonished before that his course was leading him toward danger? Was it a single offense or was it committed more than once? Was his confession voluntary or did he have to be accused by others before confessing? And, above all, does he show true repentance and manifest a heartfelt desire to avoid any repetition of the wrong?

If we are to continue showing mercy to an offender, sincere repentance is a vital factor. (2 Chron. 7:14; Isa. 55:7; Ezek. 18:30, 31) Not everyone, of course, will manifest his sorrow over the wrong in the same manner. But the elders should look for evidence that the sorrow is of a godly kind, distinguishing this from mere regret over being found out or because of having to bear a measure of shame or having one's reputation suffer damage. They can be guided by the fine description given at 2 Corinthians 7:9-11. The sadness should be over having done wrong to begin with, for having shown disrespect for the heavenly Father's will and thus having damaged one's relationship *with Him.* Of course, the individual who truly appreciates privileges of service and the esteem of his brothers would naturally also regret any loss in this regard. But his sorrow springs from the right source: genuine repentance, rejecting the wrong as detestable, sincerely regretting that he ever did it.

Some may manifest this repentance right after committing the wrong; others may do so later. Some may do so even during the course of meeting with the judicial committee. The elders' remarks at that time may bring home to the offender the real badness of his act, so he 'listens to them.'—Matt. 18:17.

In the case of a genuinely repentant wrongdoer, what then? Where the evidence is that a single offense is involved, that the individual had not ignored earlier admonition or reproof as to his course and that he had not 'pursued' the wrong but had been 'overtaken' in it under pressure or temptation of circumstances, the judicial committee might decide that the reproof could be given "in a spirit of mildness." (Gal. 6:1) If the person is thoroughly crushed and cut to the heart, there is no need to add to his sorrow. (1 Thess. 5:14) In trying to "readjust" such a one, the judicial committee should be sure that he clearly understands Jehovah's viewpoint of his serious wrong, but at the same time they will be concerned with helping him to draw close to God in humility and with confidence in God's mercy. (Jas. 4:8-10) Since his sin manifested spiritual weakness, they would properly remove any weight of responsibility from him in the congregation arrangement, such as that of being an elder, a ministerial servant, a pioneer or any other such responsibility though of a subordinate nature. He may continue as a congregation publisher, however. According to the gravity of the sin, they may decide that, for the present, it would be best for the spiritually weak one just to listen at the meetings, rather than having parts on the service meeting or giving talks in the Theocratic Ministry School, or commenting or offering prayer. The presiding elder of the judicial committee can notify those who preside over the meetings as to what restrictions have been decided upon. This also serves as a discipline for the wrongdoer and impresses upon him the need to respect God's holiness. (Gal. 6:7-9) Thus this form of reproof is administered without its being publicly announced "before all onlookers," namely, the assembled congregation.

The judicial committee may strongly recommend to the one thus reproved to discontinue certain associations or habits that contributed to the wrongdoing and that could lead to a repetition thereof. (1 Cor. 15:33; 2 Cor. 6:17) The repentant one should be happy to respond to these recommendations. No prohibitions or rules would be placed as to eating or drinking, though strong counsel may be given if one is immoderate in these things that were involved in the sin. The person would be free to engage fully in the preaching work and to report such; on the other hand, no requirements or quotas would be set for such activity or for meeting attendance, as these must be voluntary to be of value before God. Because of their interest in helping the repentant one to become spiritually healthy and strong again, the judicial committee will want to talk to him on several occasions to see where they can be of assistance, perhaps spending some time visiting with the person for upbuilding discussion.

As the judicial committee see evidence of his regaining spiritual strength and stability, showing genuine appreciation for God's righteous ways, they may gradually lift whatever restrictions were imposed. For example, they may invite him again to share in commenting at the meetings or in giving student talks, things wherein he speaks just for himself rather than as representing the congregation. Later, as he gives evidence of full recovery they may restore to him the privilege of sharing in parts on the service meeting program, assisting a ministerial servant in some department or, eventually, even in representing the congregation before God in prayer. If he moves to another congregation, this gradual restoration of privileges may be supervised by the judicial committee there. No time period is set for this, since it depends upon not only the gravity of the wrong but also the spiritual progress manifested by the repentant one. It may be several months, a year or even more before he is viewed as fully recovered. The elders will consider, not only what is for the good of the person thus reproved, but also what is in the best interests of the congregation.

PUBLIC REPROOF

Paul wrote to Timothy: "Reprove before all onlookers persons who *practice* sin [the ones . . . sinning, *Interlinear*] that the rest also may have fear." (1 Tim. 5:20) Therefore, when the evidence shows that the wrongdoer, though repentant, was guilty of committing the offense on more than one occasion, the congregation as a whole should be informed, thus openly reproving the wrongdoer. In the case of a single act, however, what if the wrongdoer not only failed to come forward with a voluntary confession about it, but also failed to heed admonitions and had been 'courting' danger by a measure of loose conduct? Or what if his wrong has become public knowledge or is such as would readily become a subject for discussion by members of the congregation? This, too, would make it advisable to make an announcement to the congregation.

In making the announcement it may simply be stated that the person named has engaged in "conduct unbecoming a Christian" and then it could be explained that he will not be sharing in certain privileges, listing these according to what the judicial committee decides in his particular case. Where the wrong has become public knowledge, this announcement will provide the brothers with a means to defend before critics the congregation as holding to right standards; it will also reduce the likelihood of unprofitable and damaging gossip. Though this is a more severe reproof, it is for the good of the offender and of the congregation as a whole, working to counteract any influences leading to a recurrence of the wrong, and enabling all in the congregation to avoid being a cause for temptation to him.

On the offender's part, he should appreciate the healthful benefits and wisdom of such discipline and not "belittle" it or "give out" under such correction. It is evidence that both God and the congregation want to 'gain' him back from a course that could lead to destruction.—Heb. 12:5-13, 15-17.

Whether such announcement is made as a reproof to the wrongdoer before the congregation as a whole or not, when privileges are restored to such a person upon his progressing in a spiritual recovery, there is no need to announce such restoration of privileges. The ones presiding at meetings should be advised, of course, but the rest of the congregation will become aware of this as they see him commenting again at meetings, acting as a householder in a demonstration or giving student talks, and so forth. If the publicly reproved individual moves to another congregation during the time that there are still restrictions imposed on him, the judicial committee that handled the case should notify the judicial committee of the congregation to which he moves, doing so through the presiding overseer there. Then those elders may supervise the gradual return of privileges to him.

Everything should be done with a purpose, keeping clearly in focus the two major concerns of the elders: to help to restore and "readjust" the wrongdoer, and to protect the cleanness and spiritual health of the congregation.

If the person was serving as an elder or a ministerial servant when he committed a serious wrong even though it was some years ago, he bears a degree of reprehensibility, for he continued to serve in that position though knowing that he had, for the time at least, disqualified himself, not being then "free from accusation." (1 Tim. 3:2, 10; Titus 1:6, 7) He should have informed the judicial committee that he did not adhere to the requirements and should have stepped down from his position. In view of his failure to do this at that time, he would now be removed from that position.

In any case where persons serving as elders or ministerial servants, or having appointments as regular or special pioneers, commit serious wrongs and are therefore put under any restrictions by a judicial committee, notification of this should be sent to the branch office so that the records there can be adjusted accordingly. As regards pioneers removed for such reason, the branch office will receive future applications to pioneer only after a period of at least a year, if they are then recommended by the judicial committee.

DISFELLOWSHIPING

What if the merciful efforts of the elders fail to 'gain' the brother? If he shows himself lacking in genuine repentance, whether he committed the serious sin only once or was a practicer of sin, then they cannot continue dealing with him in mercy, for this would show disrespect for God's standards of righteousness and holiness. Moreover, he would be a danger to the congregation, for he gives no genuine assurance that he will not continue in his wrong course. He must then

be disfellowshiped, cut off from the congregation.
—1 Cor. 5:9-13.

In view of the fact that repentance (accompanied by a 'turning around' from the wrong way) is what determines whether the person merits disfellowshiping or not, the committee must be particularly careful in accepting as genuine any "repentance" on the part of a person where the evidence has shown him guilty of evasive lying, deceit, or even collusion in connection with his wrongdoing.

In all cases of disfellowshiping the congregation committee should draw up an announcement to be read to the congregation. It may simply state that the person named has been disfellowshiped from the congregation due to "conduct unbecoming a Christian."

Some baptized persons may join a secular organization the principles of which are opposed to the Scriptural principles on which the Christian congregation is based. (Dan. 2:44; Matt. 4:8, 9; John 6:15; Isa. 2:2-4) By such action, the individual is repudiating the congregation of Jehovah's witnesses with which he associated. The judicial committee should endeavor to find out the facts that prove that he has of his own accord disassociated himself from the congregation. They should announce this fact to the congregation so that all will know the decision the person has taken. All that needs to be said is that the person "by his course of conduct has disassociated himself from the congregation of Jehovah's people."

In all cases of disfellowshiping and disassociation the branch office should be notified, and a copy of the letter of notification should be retained in the congregation files. The judicial committee should give the date the action was taken, the ground and a brief review of the evidence for it, and each member of the judicial committee should sign the letter.

Being disfellowshiped is a serious matter. One who is disfellowshiped is in a very different situation from that of the person described at 2 Thessalonians 3:14, 15 which says: "But if anyone is not obedient to our word through this letter, keep this one marked, stop associating with him, that he may become ashamed. And yet do not be considering him as an enemy, but continue admonishing him as a brother." This latter "marked" one was failing to respond to apostolic exhortation and instructions, not acting in an orderly manner, perhaps not working to support himself or idly meddling in matters not of his concern. Still he had not committed any wrongdoing of sufficient gravity to merit disfellowshiping. However, he was to be "marked," that is, identified by the individual members of the congregation as poor company, a poor example. (Compare verse 6.) The brothers in the congregation should stop associating intimately with him, that is, not have social connections with him or seek his company. Yet they would not view him as expelled from the congregation or an enemy but would "continue admonishing him as a brother."

On the other hand, one committing grave wrongs and who, due to not having repented, must be disfellowshiped is no longer recognized as a member of the congregation, as a "brother." The faithful members of the congregation not only "quit mixing in company" with him (this term being the same in Greek as that translated "stop associating" in 2 Thessalonians 3:14) but they go farther. They follow the instruction to "remove the wicked man from among yourselves."—1 Cor. 5:5, 11-13; 1 Tim. 1:19, 20.

Any baptized person who deliberately pursues a course of immoral conduct is actually rejecting the teachings of the Bible, just as much so as one who teaches others contrary to what the Scriptures say about the identity of God, the provision of the ransom, the resurrection, and so forth. (Compare Titus 3:10, 11; 2 Timothy 2:16-19.) Concerning such persons God's Word counsels: "Everyone that pushes ahead and does not remain in the teaching of the Christ does not have God. . . . If anyone comes to you and does not bring this teaching, never receive him into your homes or say a greeting to him. For he that says a greeting to him is a sharer in his wicked works." (2 John 9-11) In faithfulness to God, none in the congregation should greet such persons when meeting them in public nor should they welcome these into their homes.

Even blood relatives who do not live in the same home with a disfellowshiped relative, because of valuing spiritual relationships more than fleshly ones, avoid contact with such disfellowshiped relative just as much as possible. (Luke 8:19-21; 14:26) And those who may be members of the same household with a disfellowshiped person cease sharing spiritual fellowship with the unrepentant wrongdoer. In this way the wrongdoer is made to feel the enormity of his wrong, and, at the same time, Jehovah upholds the good name of his earthly organization and protects the spiritual well-being of his servants on earth.

This does not mean that parents would stop counseling or disciplining a baptized child who had been disfellowshiped and who was living in the same home with them. Since the true basis for discipline and training is God's Word, they would properly give their son or daughter strong counsel from that Word as necessary. This, however, does not mean fellowshiping spiritually with the child in a regular study in which he is viewed as an approved sharer. To share in such family studies, the child would first have to show repentance and change and be reinstated by the judicial committee.

Similarly a married person whose mate has been disfellowshiped, being "one flesh" with that person, may encourage the disfellowshiped one to turn around from his wrong course and repentantly seek acceptance back into the congregation. Again, this does not mean sitting down with the mate in a family study of the Bible and fellowshiping in that way. Rather, what is said constitutes a call to repentance.

But in any such case, there is no reason to listen to a disfellowshiped child or mate if such one attempts to justify himself or endeavors to sway the faithful one to his way of thinking and acting. Nor should he be listened to regarding objections as to the handling of his case by the judicial committee. If he wants to appeal his case he should go to them, not try to appeal by pleading his case with those not elders.

An elder may be approached by a disfellowshiped person who wishes to talk with him. In such case, the elder may explain to the person what he needs to do to be accepted again into the congregation, pointing out to him the need for seeking to regain a fine relationship with God, searching the Scriptures and attending all meetings open to him. This does not mean listening to a review of the case from the person, since one elder could not properly reach a conclusion unilaterally anyway. Out of respect for the arrangement of the body of elders, the one approached would direct the disfellowshiped person to the judicial committee for spiritual help and counsel in his seeking to be reinstated in the congregation.

A disfellowshiped person is not prohibited from attending meetings in the Kingdom Hall open to the general public as long as he conducts himself properly. None will greet him, of course, and he may not attend any meetings held in private homes. The congregation will not assign him any territory nor accept field service reports from him. He may obtain copies of the Society's publications for personal use. Perhaps what he reads will help to correct his thinking, soften his heart and move him to turn back to Jehovah.

Some baptized persons may cease to associate actively with a congregation, no longer meeting with their brothers. They may later become involved in serious wrongdoing. The congregation elders should take note of that fact, as they have the responsibility of doing what is necessary to maintain or clear the congregation's name for cleanness and to safeguard its right standing with God. The fact that he has isolated himself would not affect the judicial committee as to taking the steps already discussed for dealing with wrongdoers.

NONBAPTIZED ASSOCIATES WHO ARE WRONGDOERS

What of unbaptized persons who have been regularly associating with the congregation but who now become involved in serious wrongdoing? They should be dealt with in a way similar to that in the case of baptized persons, with the exception that, not being recognized members of the congregation, they would not be formally expelled therefrom. It may be that they do not understand fully the Bible's standards, and kind counsel may help them to make straight paths for their feet. Nevertheless, if they are not repentant and fail to turn from their wrongdoing, then the congregation should be advised that their conduct is "unbecoming a Christian" and that association with them would not be in harmony with the counsel at 1 Corinthians 15:33. No field service reports would be accepted from such ones.

DEALING WITH MINOR CHILDREN
AND MARRIED COUPLES

A baptized child's being a minor does not shield him from reproof before the congregation by the elders, or disfellowshiping, if he commits serious wrongdoing. In minor trespasses, of course, the child would be counseled and reproved by his parents, particularly the father, with whom the responsibility for rearing and training the children rests. (Eph. 6:4; Col. 3:20; Heb. 12:9) However, where wrongdoing becomes a practice, or is of a serious nature, such as gross loose conduct or fornication, or is such that brings the congregation into a bad light in the community, then the elders rightly are concerned. The brothers serving in judicial capacity should arrange to meet with the baptized minor to see what can be done to correct the situation, and it would be most advisable for the parents also to be present to hear what is said. If reproof and discipline are necessary, these should be given to the minor, in some cases publicly, according to the gravity of the wrongdoing and the extent to which it has affected the congregation or become known. As a baptized member of the congregation, he is a disciple and has accepted the headship of Christ Jesus.—Matt. 28:19, 20.

Of course, the elders are particularly desirous of 'gaining' the young brother or sister and in their efforts to do so they will seek the cooperation of the parents, working through them in all ways possible. Thus there will be a harmonious coordination of authority, that of the judicial committee as shepherds under Christ Jesus and that of the parents as the ones through whom the child received life and as the ones divinely appointed to bring up the child "in the discipline and mental-regulating of Jehovah." (Eph. 6:4) If the baptized child is unrepentant or still persists in a wrong course, then he should be disfellowshiped.

These same principles would apply in the case of an unbaptized minor who regularly associates with the congregation, with the exception that, in the event of his becoming an unrepentant wrongdoer, no formal disfellowshiping would be made. But an announcement would be made, enabling the congregation to safeguard itself against harm.

Parents should cooperate with the judicial committee in their responsibility to shepherd the congregation. While the law set forth at Deuteronomy 21:18-21 obviously does not refer to small children (since it speaks of a son who becomes "a glutton and a drunkard"), it does set the precedent of placing the spiritual interests and safety of God's congregation above family relationships. Parents who love God and their brothers will not cover up or excuse continued or flagrant sinning on the part of their children.

As to married couples, elders ought to be careful not to intervene unnecessarily in the affairs of such. If their assistance and spiritual help are asked, they may offer appropriate counsel. However, when serious wrongdoing occurs, then, of course, the judicial committee is responsible to do what is necessary to safeguard the cleanness of the congregation as well as to seek to effect the restoration of the offender. They would counsel, reprove or disfellowship either mate as necessary. At the same time, where the offender is the wife they will seek to coordinate their shepherding work with the baptized husband's exercise of headship over his wife, maintaining a harmonious coordination of authority, working through the husband as far as is possible. If the husband is the offender, then, of course, the giving of admonition and correction will rest with the judicial committee, in view of the wife's subordinate position. Their limiting either mate's participation in meetings, or similar activity, would depend upon the same factors discussed earlier, as would the decision as to whether announcement should be made of their taking such action.

REINSTATING REPENTANT DISFELLOWSHIPED PERSONS

Paul's second letter to the Corinthians, evidently written some months after his first, called on the Corinthian congregation to restore the man they had disfellowshiped, in view of his repentance and deep sorrow. (2 Cor. 2:6-8) So, it may be several months, a year or even years before a disfellowshiped person gives convincing evidence of repentance. This genuine repentance and abandonment of the wrong course is always the determining factor, not the specific act committed nor merely the time that has elapsed. (Compare 1 Corinthians 5:1.) Of course, where there was evidence of lying, deceit or conspiracy in connection with the wrongdoing, or even evidence of such on the part of the offender during the judicial hearings, then the judicial committee should exercise special care and caution not to be deceived into accepting back one who is not truly and genuinely repentant.

When the judicial committee believes that a disfellowshiped person is truly repentant, they may prepare an announcement of his reinstatement to be read to the congregation. They should also advise the branch office of this action.

How should the reinstated person be received by the congregation? Though the disfellowshiped man in Corinth, to whom Paul made reference, had brought reproach on the congregation there and caused them sorrow, they were instructed by the apostle that they should "kindly forgive" him for this and "comfort him," confirming their love for him. (2 Cor. 2:5-8) Of course, such person, though now received back as a brother, is still not spiritually strong. So, he needs to be concentrating on building himself up, and being built up, through his association. In course of time the judicial committee may feel that he has progressed to the point of again sharing in commenting in the meetings, and thereafter they may gradually let him do more as he gives evidence of progress toward spiritual strength and stability. A year or even more may pass, however, before he is called on to take a part in a congregation program or to represent the congregation in prayer before God or otherwise serve in any representative capacity.

Could one who has been disfellowshiped ever be appointed as a ministerial servant or even as an elder? This would depend upon his being able to reach the standing of being "irreprehensible," having "a fine testimony from people on the outside," "free from accusation," along with manifesting the other qualities required. (1 Tim. 3:2, 7, 10; Titus 1:6, 7) He would have to 'live down' the reproach he brought on himself by his wrong act, doing this by building up a convincing record of righteousness that would serve to counterbalance the effect of the past wrong. This might take five, ten or fifteen years to do, depending upon the gravity of the wrongdoing. In some cases where great scandal resulted, he might not be able to live it down sufficiently in his lifetime so as to qualify for serving as an elder.

The same need to regain a fine reputation for righteousness before being recommended to serve in such positions would apply to men who committed serious wrongdoing but were not disfellowshiped due to sincere repentance.

The action taken by the judicial committee of any one congregation is to be respected by all other congregations, thereby maintaining unity under Christ's headship. If a disfellowshiped person moves to the territory of another congregation, an announcement should there be made of his disfellowshiped status. If he seeks reinstatement, the matter should be handled through the congregation that disfellowshiped him. This is because the circumstances that led to his disfellowshiping are best known there. So, the judicial committee of the congregation in whose territory he is currently located could hear his plea for reinstatement, consider the evidence of his sincere repentance and his following a right course, and could then make their recommendation, giving their reasons, to the congregation that first handled the case. Then a decision could be made by the now-existing judicial committee of that first congregation. This should be done wherever possible, but good judgment must be used.

APPEALING DECISIONS
OF A JUDICIAL COMMITTEE

If one who is disfellowshiped believes that an error in judgment was committed, he may appeal to the body of elders for a rehearing of the matter, just as soon as possible, doing so in writing. In such case, it would seem good that the appeal be heard by another judicial committee, perhaps three other elders from that congregation, if available. It may be preferable, however, to invite three elders from nearby congregations to serve, particularly if the disfellowshiped person has raised a complaint of partiality. It is suggested that the presiding overseer of the congregation write to the branch office in his country, as the office may be able to recommend certain elders to serve in this way or may even find it advisable to have one or more circuit or district overseers help out in hearing the appeal in certain cases.

Where an appeal is heard, it is necessary to rehear all the evidence previously presented as well as any additional testimony that the one requesting the appeal hearing, or the elders of the congregation, may wish to offer. Wherever possible, the judicial committee that heard the original case should also be present at the appeal and furnish the appeal committee whatever written records they have of the first hearing. If they believe that earlier testimony is being changed, they can so state, their testimony being heard by the appeal committee. The appeal committee may also wish to question them as to their reasons for reaching the conclusion they did.

Whatever the appeal committee decides, either agreeing with the disfellowshiping action or disallowing it, and thereby canceling it, their decision will be final. And, since the matter will now have been heard by at least six different elders, there is no reason to consider any further appeal.

RESPONSIBILITY OF ALL ELDERS A WEIGHTY ONE

It can be seen from all this that the congregation elders have a weighty responsibility to bear. While some are assigned to serve as a judicial committee during the course of the year, all elders are to be men who, as shepherds, protect the flock from harm. (Acts 20:28-31) Each should be able "to exhort by the teaching that is healthful and to reprove those who contradict," whether such contradiction be by word, action or spirit. (Titus 1:9-14) They should manifest, not "a spirit of cowardice, but that of power and of love and of soundness of mind." (2 Tim. 1:7) Rather than wait until things reach a crisis stage, they should try to meet problems early, 'reprimanding, exhorting, with all long-suffering and art of teaching.' (2 Tim. 4:1-5) By faithfulness in doing this, they will 'save both themselves and those who listen to them.'—1 Tim. 4:6, 10, 11, 16.

When difficulties arise or cases of wrongdoing must be dealt with, they will keep in mind Paul's words to Timothy, also an overseer: "I solemnly charge you before God and Christ Jesus and the chosen angels to keep these things without prejudgment, doing nothing according to a biased leaning." (1 Tim. 5:21) They should deal impartially, showing no bias for or against anyone, never letting fleshly relationships or personal friendships or class distinctions becloud their vision or cause them to manifest prejudice or favoritism in their judgment.—Lev. 19:15; Deut. 1:17; 10:17, 18; Jas. 2:1-9; 1 Pet. 1:17.

Like Israel's high priest, they should be able to "deal moderately with the ignorant and erring ones," realizing that they themselves are imperfect. (Heb. 5:2) Knowing that it is 'the merciful who will be shown mercy,' they should seek to imitate Jehovah and his Son in this admirable quality, not dealing harshly with their brothers but mercifully seeking to 'gain' erring ones, and instructing with mildness those not favorably disposed, or who for a time betray wrong thinking and wrong understanding. (2 Tim. 2:23-26) At the same time they should never be disloyal to God or show disrespect for his holiness, nor manifest a lack of love for their brothers by allowing wrongdoers to go uncorrected or unreproved, or by allowing corrupting influences to infiltrate the congregation.—Compare 1 Samuel 2:12-17, 27-30; Malachi 2:8, 9; Jude 3, 4.

EACH ONE'S PART IN SAFEGUARDING THE CLEANNESS OF THE CONGREGATION

The responsibility for maintaining cleanness in the congregation is not solely that of the overseers. To all of us who have hope of life in God's new order the words apply: "Therefore, since we have these promises, beloved ones, let us cleanse ourselves of every defilement of flesh and spirit, perfecting holiness in God's fear."—2 Cor. 7:1.

You help to promote moral cleanness of the congregation by your own personal conduct, which may move observers on the outside to glorify God. (1 Pet. 2:12) When you resist temptation to wrongdoing you are contributing to the moral cleanness of the congregation earth wide. The same is true when you refuse to feed your mind on ideas that stimulate wrong desires. (Matt. 5:27-30; Phil. 4:8, 9) Parents, by properly training and disciplining their children so that they walk in the paths of righteousness, contribute to the fine reputation of Jehovah's people. So do younger persons, by obedience to their parents and by refusing to imitate the world and its ways. (Compare Luke 2:51, 52.) When you take care to teach interested persons the Bible's high moral standards before they get baptized, this, too, acts to keep the entire Christian congregation earth wide clean. These are things that it is most important to do, so that the spirit of God may continue to operate freely on the congregation.—1 Cor. 5:5; 1 Thess. 5:23.

If you personally are ever a witness to serious wrongdoing on the part of a baptized member of the congregation or an unbaptized person regularly associated with it, loyalty to Jehovah and his Son and love for your brothers should move you to bring the matter to the attention of the judicial committee. (Ps. 31:23) It is no real kindness to the wrongdoer to conceal his unchristian conduct; it may only contribute to his becoming hardened in sin to the point where he cannot turn back, and so lead to his everlasting destruction. Certainly it shows no love for Jehovah God or his people when one becomes a party to wickedness by concealing those who practice it. (Deut. 13:6-8) In ancient Israel a public curse was pronounced on any who, knowing the facts of a certain wrongdoing or crime, failed to come forward with such testimony. (Lev. 5:1; Prov. 29:24) One who loves righteousness and is truly loyal to Jehovah God and Christ Jesus will courageously step forward and make known the sinful conduct and conscientiously testify to the truth of the matter before the judicial committee when called on to do so.—Ex. 23:2, 3.

You also contribute to the spiritual health of the congregation by showing respect for decisions of the congregation judicial committee. (Compare Numbers 16: 41-50.) Realize that, not having heard all the testimony and evidence that these have heard, you are certainly not in the same position as they are for reaching a right conclusion.

Our learning to live now in harmony with Jehovah's requirements, maintaining cleanness in teaching and conduct, is preparation for life in God's new system of things. Therefore it is vital for each one of us to impress God's righteous precepts on his mind and heart.

Accurate knowledge of God's law will safeguard us against bringing great grief upon both ourselves and others because of ignorance. And love for what Jehovah shows us to be right will motivate us to act in harmony with it.

CHAPTER 10

ENDURANCE THAT RESULTS IN DIVINE APPROVAL

"YOU have need of endurance," wrote the apostle Paul, "in order that, after you have done the will of God, you may receive the fulfillment of the promise." —Heb. 10:36.

Thanks to Jehovah's undeserved kindness, we have been privileged to become baptized disciples of the Lord Jesus Christ. Our life now has purposeful direction, we enjoy a clean standing before Jehovah God, we have freeness of speech in approaching him in prayer, and before us lies the prospect of endless life as his devoted servants.

But will we gain the "fulfillment of the promise"? We will, only if we endure. Endurance is a quality that must be developed and we do that by having our faith put to the test and then holding firmly to that faith. "Consider it all joy, my brothers, when you meet with various trials, knowing as you do that this tested quality of your faith works out endurance. But let endurance have its work complete, that you may be complete and sound in all respects, not lacking in anything." (Jas. 1:2-4) God's adversary and those dominated by him will bring experiences upon you designed to tear you down. Human imperfections, on the part of ourselves and others, may produce trials. But James' words show that these very things can, in fact, build you up, yes, produce in you the quality you need in order to win Jehovah's approval. (Rom. 5:3, 4) What a happy reversal of matters that is! How, then, can we let endurance "have its work complete"?

We must, first of all, endure in Christian living, in loyally and courageously producing the fruits of God's spirit. Without that all our preaching and teaching would become meaningless. Nothing gives greater force to the proclamation of Bible truth than backing it up with a praiseworthy example.—Compare Romans 2:21-23.

Do we truly believe that God's kingdom is the best government for mankind, and do we want others to recognize that we are sincere in advocating its rule? Then we must uphold the law of the appointed King, uphold the 'law of Christ' based on love of God and of our neighbor. (Matt. 22:37-40; Gal. 6:2) It is our intense love for our brothers that proves our love for God; it is the mark distinguishing us as genuine disciples of his Son. (John 13:34, 35) Do people on the outside see this distinguishing mark in us? Are we consistent in manifesting that love? Will we express it, if need be, even to the point of surrendering our lives on behalf of our brothers, as God's Son "surrendered his soul for us"? —1 John 3:16; 4:20, 21.

We cannot wait until a major crisis severely tests our love for our brothers. Rather, it is a matter of each day, and day by day, proving our love for them, not giving up in manifesting genuine concern for them. Elders and ministerial servants must not "tire out" in doing what is fine on behalf of their brothers, nor should any of us. (Gal. 6:9, 10) If, for example, we were to neglect those who are aged, infirm or sick among us, failing to visit and help them, would not observers outside the congregation have reason to question the genuineness of our Christian discipleship? Would this not seriously weaken the force of our preaching?

Pressures and tensions created by the present system of things can only be expected to grow. We must endure in fine works in the face of these adverse forces, not letting them cause us to become callous or indifferent or to grow irritated and contentious. If disparaging gossip or backbiting were to creep into the congregation, would not honest-hearted persons seriously wonder if they should continue associating with people who do not practice what they preach? (Eph. 4:25, 29; Jas. 3:8-12) We must steadfastly "pursue the things making for peace and the things that are upbuilding to one another." This includes not letting such things as our choice of food, drink, entertainment, dress or appearance ever become a cause for stumbling to others. Rather, "let each of us please his neighbor in what is good for his upbuilding. For even Christ did not please himself." (Rom. 14:19-21; 15:1-3) How sad it would be if weak ones were to be lopped off by the adversary because those of us who are stronger were inconsiderate or neglected to help them! This would defeat the very purpose of the disciple-making work, namely, to aid as many as possible to gain Jehovah's approval and life.

At the same time, endurance in the 'law of Christ' will keep us from becoming unnecessarily critical of our brothers, from making issues of matters of a purely personal nature. (Rom. 14:10-12) Jesus said: "My yoke is kindly and my load is light." (Matt. 11:30) We should not make endurance under that yoke and load a burdensome thing by trying to impose on others standards that express only our personal preference and opinion, not being stated in God's Word.

EVERY ASPECT OF LIFE INVOLVED

Jehovah's people earth wide are under scrutiny. When we are preaching and teaching, also in our homes, at our jobs, at school, in all our daily contacts, people note not only our words but our actions and ways. What kind of reputation do we individually have among people outside the Christian congregation? Does our home, by its neatness and cleanness, represent the God of holiness whom we serve? Do we reflect the wisdom of God's Word and its ability to produce harmonious marriages and happy families? Do our children manifest the wholesome effects of the "discipline and mental-regulating of Jehovah" by their manners and conduct? (Eph. 5:21–6:4) Are we known by employers, officials or teachers as persons who consistently uphold right principles?

Really, if any of us should be viewed by others as lazy, sloppy, uncooperative, careless, rude or undependable, would we not be deterring people from investigating the truth we proclaim? But if we are known as considerate, reasonable, helpful, trustworthy and upright, then they have evidence that Christ's kingdom rule does indeed produce better people. And they may themselves become glorifiers of Jehovah.—1 Pet. 2:12.

May our example of endurance in right ways, then, demonstrate to honest-hearted ones that submission to the 'law of Christ' is the best way of life. True, being imperfect, we may at times find ourselves falling short in this; but we should not become discouraged. Transforming one's life as a disciple of Christ is a continuing process; it is not completed at the time of water baptism. (Eph. 4:20-24) God's spirit will continue to help us to make improvement if we persist in seeking his help, not giving up.—Matt. 7:7, 8; Luke 18:1.

GAINING THE VICTORY IN SPIRITUAL WARFARE

Never lose sight of the fact that you are in a spiritual warfare. To come off victorious you must make full use of the provisions Jehovah has made. You need to "go on acquiring power in the Lord and in the mightiness of his strength." (Eph. 6:10-13) How can this be done?

Daily study and meditation on God's Word will help to fortify your mind and heart, will aid you to make decisions always in harmony with God's will. Regular association with Jehovah's devoted people in meetings will prevent your getting into a position where, by being alone, you are easy prey for the enemy. Regular participation in the preaching and disciple-making work is likewise strengthening; it will keep you from becoming self-centered or from becoming unfeeling toward all those in the world of mankind whose lives are now in grave danger due to the swift approach of the "great tribulation." (Matt. 24:21, 38, 39; 2 Thess. 1:6-10) Obedience to the 'law of Christ' requires that you zealously and courageously give the warning and work toward the salvation of all who will give heed. No matter what the reaction or response of people in your territory, strong love for God and an earnest desire to see his name magnified will stimulate you to press forward in his service, in imitation of Jesus Christ. —John 17:4.

Severe tests of your devotion may come from sources very close to you, from members of your own family. You must then face the question: Which is the stronger tie, the controlling one in your life? It truly must be your love of God and Christ. (Matt. 10:32-39) Though maintaining endurance may seem extremely difficult in such cases, remember: For you to forsake God or disobey him is not going to bring benefits to anyone. Jesus said that "by endurance on your part you will acquire your souls." And by refusing to become a quitter you keep from removing from your home the fine influence that can aid others there also to gain salvation. —Luke 21:19; 1 Cor. 7:16.

The psalmist David wrote: "In case my own father and my own mother did leave me, even Jehovah himself would take me up." (Ps. 27:10) As a disciple of the Lord Jesus Christ you enjoy association with a large family under the loving headship of Jehovah God. So, you need never lack for encouraging, joyful and strengthening fellowship that will help you to endure with life everlasting in view.—Mark 10:29, 30.

The spirit of nationalism is strong throughout the earth in our day. After expressing God's view of today's situation, the prophetic vision adds: "Here is where it means endurance for the holy ones, those who observe the commandments of God and the faith of Jesus." (Rev. 14:9-12) The "holy ones" have repeatedly had their faith tested on this issue, and their "other sheep" companions are now being called on to manifest the same unbreakable integrity and faithful endurance in connection therewith.

Tests may come because of wars, revolutions or outright persecution and official bans, and these may make it impossible for you to carry on Christian worship in all the detailed ways suggested in this book. It may be impossible to hold large congregation meetings. Contact with the branch office may temporarily be broken off. Visits by circuit overseers may be interrupted. New publications may not arrive. If any of these things happens to you, what should you do?

The answer is: Do whatever you can, and as much as you can, in the way of pure worship under the circumstances. Personal study should be possible. Usually small groups of brothers can meet for study in homes. Publications studied in the past, and the Bible itself, can be used as a basis for meetings. Do not become excited or worried. Generally in a short time some form of communication with an agency of the governing body will be established, because the governing body always seeks to find ways of getting in touch with the brothers.

But even if you find yourself isolated from all your Christian brothers, keep in mind that you are not isolated from Jehovah and his Son Jesus Christ. Jehovah can still hear your prayers and he can strengthen you with his spirit. Look to him for guidance. Remember that you are a servant of Jehovah and a disciple of Jesus Christ, and, as opportunities to witness to others open up, make good use of them. Jehovah will bless your efforts and others may soon join you in worship. —Phil. 1:27-30; 4:6, 7; 2 Tim. 4:16-18; Acts 4:13-31; 5:27-42.

Although, like the apostles and others, you should be faced with the very threat of death, put strong trust in "the God who raises up the dead." (2 Cor. 1:8-10) Your faith in his provision of the resurrection can help you to endure even the most severe opposition. (Luke 21:19) Christ Jesus set the example; he knew that his faithfulness under test would strengthen others to endure. You, too, can be a source of strength to your brothers in a similar way.—John 16:33; Heb. 12:2, 3; 1 Pet. 2:21.

We must always maintain union with our appointed Head, Christ Jesus. We need to work closely with the "faithful and discreet slave" and its governing body, which Jesus uses to accomplish his Father's will. We need to make full use of the privilege of prayer. Remember, no prison walls or solitary confinement can cut off our communication with the Supreme Judge of all the earth.

With determination and endurance let us persevere in the work that the resurrected Jesus Christ set out for all his disciples: "Go therefore and make disciples of people of all the nations, baptizing them in the name of the Father and of the Son and of the holy spirit, teaching them to observe all the things I have commanded you." (Matt. 28:19, 20) It is our privilege as baptized disciples of Christ to share in carrying out his prophecy, which has a major fulfillment in this "conclusion of the system of things," namely: "And this good news of the kingdom will be preached in all the inhabited earth for a witness to all the nations; and then the end will come." (Matt. 24:3, 14) Having applied ourselves wholeheartedly in that work during this period of time as a theocratic organization, we will be blessed with the opportunity to serve Jehovah everlastingly in his righteous new order.

INDEX

DESIGNATIONS OF BIBLE TRANSLATIONS
QUOTED OR CITED HEREIN

AV — *Authorized* or *King James Version* (1611).

AT — *The Bible · An American Translation* (1935), J. M. P. Smith and E. J. Goodspeed.

Dy — Catholic *Douay Version* (1610).

Int — *The Kingdom Interlinear Translation of the Greek Scriptures* (1969).

Je — *The Jerusalem Bible* (1966), A. Jones, general editor.

Knox — *The Holy Bible* (1955), Ronald A. Knox.

Lamsa — *The Holy Bible from Ancient Eastern Manuscripts* (1957), George M. Lamsa.

Mo — *A New Translation of the Bible* (1922), James Moffatt.

NA — *The New American Bible* (1970).

NE — *The New English Bible* (1970).

RS — *Revised Standard Version* (1952).

Schonfeld — *The Authentic New Testament* (1958), Hugh J. Schonfield.

Yg — *The Holy Bible* (1862), Robert Young.

Unless otherwise indicated, Bible quotations in this book are from the *New World Translation of the Holy Scriptures* (1971 edition).